CONSTANCE SHACKLOCK

A BIOGRAPHY

IAN THOMPSON

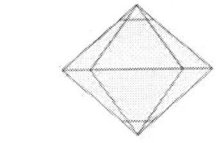

BLUESTONE BOOKS

2007

Published 2007 in Great Britain by
Bluestone Books, 259 Ashby Road, Scunthorpe
DN16 2AB

ISBN : 987-0-9537067-6-1
© Ian Thompson 2007
All rights reserved

Printed and bound in Great Britain by
BOOKSPRINT

CONTENTS

FOREWORD by James Gaddarn   page 5
PREFACE   8
Acknowledgements   11

1. Beginnings   13
2. The War Years   26
3. Let's Make an Opera Company   40
4. Enter the Maestro   58
5. A Chapter of Reviews   70
6. Tours and Visits   84
7. Artists, Accidents, Achievements   96
8. Freelance   109
9. The Sound of Music   137
10. Afterwards   144

Appendix A: *Opera Roles*   156
Appendix B: *Concert Engagements*   158
Appendix C: *Recordings*   185
Index   187

Constance c.1941, when she was a student at the Royal Academy of Music (*photo: Barron*).

FOREWORD

By JAMES GADDARN

Music lovers will, assuredly, be grateful to Mr Ian Thompson for the fascinating biography he has written to commemorate the distinguished singer Constance Shacklock who, throughout her career, was a much loved and admired member of the profession. His account of Constance's beginnings and ultimate triumphs both in the operatic and concert spheres rekindle to an older generation fond memories of a great singer. To younger enthusiasts of singing it will prove an invaluable guide to overcome potential problems on the road to success.

The possessor of a natural voice of great warmth, Constance was fortunate in studying with very fine teachers and particularly in meeting Eric Mitchell, who was her constant mentor from the time when they began to know each other until his lamented death.

How fortunate we were to hear her Brangane in the 1950s to Flagstad's Isolde; her Amneris in *Aida*, Octavian in *Der Rosenkavalier*, Azucena in *Il Trovatore* and Mrs Sedley in *Peter Grimes*. Her concert performances in the Verdi *Requiem* and *The Dream of Gerontius* thrilled audiences in London, Edinburgh, Manchester, Sheffield and Swansea.

As a founder member of the Royal Opera, Constance graduated from minor roles to stardom. She approached her work with great diligence and was gifted with a wonderful personality and communicating powers. In spite of great demands at the Opera House she also found time to give lieder recitals all over the country – her programmes invariably including the better known arias from opera, to the delight of the large audiences which she attracted on her visits to provincial cities.

After withdrawing from Covent Garden she accepted many invitations to sing in continental opera houses with great success. She caused some surprise in accepting the part of the Mother Superior in *The Sound of Music* and performed this role for some six years to the delight of many thousands of people.

I admired her work enormously and attended many of her performances. She graciously accepted my invitation to take on the role of narrator in a concert performance of Purcell's *King Arthur* on the South Bank in 1987, and proved a great success.

It is a matter of great regret that Constance made very few recordings. Fortunately there are tapes of her Brangane and the Mother Superior in *The Sound of Music.*, and one or two other things.

In her later years she was blessed in knowing Jean Tredaway: a most talented young singer whose gifts she nurtured to a very high standard. Constance subsequently adopted Jean. They supported each other marvellously and Jean's love contributed much to Constance's final years.

I have the happiest memories of them both.

James Gaddam

PREFACE

In the world of music only the great composers are truly immortal. Great soloists and great singers are gradually forgotten, or, if their names survive, it is rather as disembodied ghosts than as living legends. Melba... Caruso... Gervase Elwes...

Constance Shacklock is by no means yet a mere name. Some readers may be surprised to learn that she died as recently as 1999. Older members of the music-loving public still remember her performances with pleasure and affection and will often express their regret that so little has been done to celebrate her achievements or to prolong her memory. It is late in the day to tell her story but not, I hope, too late.

How important was she? The legendary conductor Erich Kleiber thought her the best operatic mezzo in the world, and in three or four of her operatic roles she was widely recognized as being at least on a par with the best. Her career encompassed an impressive series of 'firsts'. She was a soloist in the first-ever performance in Italy of *The Dream of Gerontius* (Rome 1957); the first British singer to be a guest artist of the Wagner Society of Holland; the first to perform behind the Iron Curtain (Berlin State Opera 1951); and one of the first two (Joan Hammond being the other) to sing at the Bolshoi Theatre in Moscow. She also became an immensely popular figure at the Last Night of the Proms, leading the singing of 'Rule Britannia!' on no less than ten occasions.

Her career was however a short one – in opera and on the

concert platform effectively fifteen years. She came to prominence when she was already in her mid-thirties, and she faded from the scene while still apparently near the height of her powers and for reasons which are not entirely understood, at the relatively early age of forty-seven. Yet all of this makes her story more interesting.

Among Constance's papers is an embryonic autobiography which exists in three versions. There is, first of all, a sheaf of A4 pages in Constance's autograph, now seriously incomplete and bearing page numbers from 64 to 113, together with one or two unnumbered pages which may have been added at a slightly later date. This version, as we now have it (Text A), picks up the story of her career in July 1953 (page 64) and ends in 1996. We know that this was the year of its composition since there is a reference on page 110 to "this year, 1996" in connection with the fiftieth anniversary of the reopening of the Royal Opera House after the Second World War.

A second, complete text was produced in typescript in May 1997 and is now contained in a hardback blue folder. This version (Text B1) is an abridged transcript of Text A by one of Constance's pupils. It is a slightly more literary version, eg. occasional notes and jottings have been turned into sentences and a certain amount of material has been omitted – most of it in the interests of greater continuity. It also contains the early missing portions of Text A, or a version of them, for which we may be very thankful. Without some account of her early years, any portrait of Constance would be seriously incomplete.

This typescript version was further revised by Constance

herself. It contains many pencilled amendments, some of them amounting to the complete rewriting of certain pages; and a number of additional passages have been inserted on separate sheets (Text B2). The inference is that Constance was still working on this text when she died.

It is possible that Text A began life as an *aide memoire*. In the late summer of 1996 Constance gave a recorded interview about her life and career to the BBC Radio 3 programme *In Tune* (transmitted 13 September 1996). It seems not unreasonable to suppose that she wanted to jot things down in advance of the interview, and the coincidence of dates is suggestive. Or it could be that the interview gave her the idea for a book. Whatever the truth of the matter, Text A grew and grew, and by the time she came to finish it her thoughts were evidently turning to publication. Significantly in this respect she concludes with the words: "I dedicate this book to my [late] husband who kept a complete record of all my performances – without that record I could never have written this book – and to my dear mother, who made many sacrifices for me when I was young."

It may be asked why, in that case, no attempt has been made to tidy up the text and issue it as a book in its own right. The answer is that what Constance left behind her was not an almost finished autobiography but a work still very much in progress. Some parts of it have an enviable immediacy and are laced with delightful anecdotes; other portions are still at the stage of an early draft. More seriously – and this is something that any publisher would have pointed out to her – the work remains basically a series of personal reminiscences. What is lacking is the kind of background information which would have placed her musical career in its proper historical context. In these circumstances it seemed to me better to use what she wrote as the basis for a biography and to excerpt from the text as frequently and as generously as I could. At key moments I have always allowed Constance to speak for herself and in some places I have expanded the text by drawing on other original sources, eg. interviews which she gave, and an account of her Russian tour which she wrote for a now-defunct periodical. The pity is that she began to write when she was already, in her own words, "double *forte* plus three." Had she started ten years earlier, the finished product would probably have earned her widespread critical acclaim.

ACKNOWLEDGEMENTS

Preparation of the text for publication was overshadowed by the untimely death of Jean Tredaway, Constance's adopted daughter, at whose request I undertook to write the book and who gave me unlimited access to all Constance's papers. For Jean, the publication of a biography had become an act of posthumous gratitude to Constance, and although it is a matter of lasting regret that she did not live to see it in print, she was at least able to read and approve the draft text only weeks before she died.

I am also grateful to Jean's sister, Mrs Joan White, who intervened to lend her own support to the project in the wake of Jean's death and to maintain matters on a warmly personal footing. For practical assistance, including the provision of all but one of the photographs, my very sincere thanks both to her and to her husband Dennis.

No list of acknowledgements would be complete without mention of Katharine Greer, long-time pupil of Constance, whose tireless dedication to Constance's memory made her an ideal intermediary. It was Katharine who introduced me to Jean and made a special journey to London in order to do so. She also provided me with valuable information about Constance's last years and her special gifts as a teacher of singing. For her own special contribution to the project including practical suggestions and encouragement I am deeply grateful.

My thanks are due also to Angela Shaw of Bulwell Library and to Mrs Win Wilson of Aspley for details relating to Constance's childhood; to Mr Michael Brook and Mrs Sylvia James, who furnished me with information about Constance's musical activities in the Nottingham area; and to Simon & Schuster UK Ltd., publishers, for kind permission to quote from *Covent Garden: The Untold Story* by Norman Lebrecht, first published by them in 2000. A more detailed acknowledgement relating to this permission occurs on page 57, footnote 1.

Last of all (and last merely as a way of emphasizing his own special contribution to the book) my heartfelt thanks to James Gaddarn for writing the Foreword.

Ian Thompson   Scunthorpe, April 2007.

I

BEGINNINGS

Port Arthur Road Nottingham is a Victorian leftover: a long row of terraced housing comprising two-bedroomed workers' cottages on the east side of the street, and three-bedroomed cottages on the west side, with the third bedroom situated directly above the first, giving an oddly imposing three-storeyed frontage. On both sides of the street the front doors open directly onto the pavement. There is no plaque on the wall of number 79 (one of the three-bedroomed houses) but it was here that Constance was born on 16 April 1913. Her father was Frederick Randolph Shacklock and her mother Hilda Louise née Lucas.

Shortly after her birth the family moved to Top Valley Farm, Bestwood Park, near Bulwell[1], where the paternal grandparents were tenant farmers. Frederick, an accomplished horseman and a cavalry trainer in the South Notts Hussars, had wished to enter the police force. "He was a very handsome man and would have made a striking figure on horseback, but it was not to be. He was the eldest son, and the farm needed him." It meant a rural upbringing for Constance, and gave her a love of animals and the countryside which she was never to lose.

There were only two children of the marriage: Constance, and her sister Rosamund, who was 6½ years her junior, and this fact, and the relative isolation of the farm, conspired to make her a rather lonely child. What further increased her sense of isolation was her mother's increasing preoccupation with domestic problems. Although Constance's father survived the First World War he returned home a deeply traumatized and very sick man. Originally, in the words of his wife, "one of the most loving of husbands," he now began to suffer from terrible nightmares and violent rages. There were times when Constance and Rosamund had to be shut away in the bedroom for their own safety and to prevent them from seeing "his terrible torments". All this she remembered very vividly. "I not only feared him but, sad to say, I hated him because he seemed so cruel. It was not until many years later that I was able to understand and love him and realize that all this was the result of what he had suffered in the War.

"I remember very clearly one occasion, when Mother felt that she couldn't take any more, and left him. We went to her sister's – a good one-and-a-half hour's walk from the farm. I can see the picture now: Mother pushing little six-month old Rosamund in the pram and sobbing most of the way, and me, aged seven, hanging on to the pram handle, wondering what it was all about. We returned home about ten days later since Mother realized how much Father needed her." In fact although the doctors despaired for his future and even, at times, for his life, it was thanks to his wife's devoted care and nursing that he did gradually recover, and actually lived to be ninety.

Gradually too there came reconciliation. The love that he had been unable to give to his children he began to show to his grandchildren, and Constance recalled the touching sight of "Pop-pop on all fours, playing horses with a little one on his back chuckling with glee."

During his last illness he and Constance had many long talks and discovered a new rapport. "On one occasion he said, with deep sadness, 'You can't kill a fellow human being and be the same afterwards.' And he recalled a few horrific incidents to me ... After all those years I saw my father as he really was: a good, loving man, almost destroyed by the war."

We talk nowadays of children being scarred by their early experiences but it is easy to overstate. Moments of fear, loneliness or misery have to be set against a wider background, and to make an obvious point, there is nothing to suggest that Constance ever felt seriously insecure. Perhaps after all, these darker experiences served merely to liberate something creative within her, as seems to have been the case with the poet Wordsworth:

> Dust as we are, the immortal spirit grows
> Like harmony in music; there is a dark
> Inscrutable workmanship that reconciles
> Discordant elements, makes them cling together
> In one society. How strange, that all
> The terrors, pains, and early miseries,
> Regrets, vexations, lassitudes, interfused

> Within my mind, should e'er have borne a part,
> And that a needful part, in making up
> The calm existence that is mine, when I
> Am worthy of myself! ²

In Constance's case too, there were compensations. Although 'Sherwood', where she was born, is merely a district of Nottingham, the remnants of Sherwood Forest lie just a few miles north of Bestwood, and the legends of Robin Hood were know to her and fired her imagination from an early age. Also there was the Nottinghamshire countryside. Few people think of Nottinghamshire as an outstandingly beautiful county, but the landscape, away from the mining villages, is tranquil, intimate, and full of subtleties. This is the countryside that D.H. Lawrence knew and loved (Eastwood, where he grew up, is barely six miles from Bestwood), and its influence on Constance seems to have been almost as profound. She remembered spending "many long hours wandering through the woods with the dogs," adding, "I do not regret this period of my life because it was during these times of loneliness that I really found myself. I remember vividly the peace and calm that I experienced in company with nature: the stillness only broken by the call of a pheasant or the rustling of some small creature in a thicket. Although I was young I began to think deeply about life."

She seems to have been blessed with an unusual awareness of the empathy which can exist between man and animals, and with a keen sense of the underlying unity of things:

"I loved animals, and used to talk to them because I felt

they were my friends and understood my loneliness. This great love of nature and animals has never left me – somehow there is an understanding between us which one cannot put into words. I long that all people could feel this. They are an integral part of creation and I believe what Albert Schweitzer wrote: 'Until we extend our circle of compassion to encompass every living creature, we shall not enjoy world peace.'"

SCHOOL DAYS

"To get to my school, which was an ordinary little council school and the nearest one to home, [3] was a good forty minutes walk, across three fields, over a level crossing and past a wagon works; so I had plenty of exercise, sometimes not very pleasant in heavy rain or snow. However it made me a very healthy girl. Just before the wagon works there was a very large oak tree with a small hole at the bottom. Here I kept a duster so that I could clean my shoes, which got very muddy walking over the fields. It became quite a joke for the men at the wagon works to enquire why, every morning, I disappeared behind the tree!

"Near to the wagon works was a private tennis court in one of the fields. At this point, when I was on my way home from school, I would shout at the top of my voice, 'COO—EE! Within a very short time my three pet geese (Pip, Squeak and Wilfred) would come running over the brow of the hill to meet me, honking loudly and flapping their wings. Tennis players, if they saw the geese coming, tended to beat a hasty retreat into the club house.

"Later on I went to a school in Nottingham: Huntingdon Street. I don't think I was a very bright student, except in music, drama and sport, because I was very undisciplined in the subjects I didn't like. I remember vividly the headmistress, Miss Partridge, saying to my mother, apropos my great success in the annual sports: 'If she were as dedicated in all her subjects as she is in sport, she would be brilliant!' "

Constance's father had been brought up in the Church of England; her mother as a Methodist; and it was to the small Methodist church in Broomhill Road, Bulwell, that she was taken by her mother – evidently to a concert – on the occasion of a chapel anniversary. "I must have decided there and then that this was the church for me because I started to go to the Sunday school and the following year I was on the platform singing a solo... As I grew older I became a choir member and a Sunday school teacher. The choir master, Mr Powell, and the organist, Charles Jones, were very kind to me. I think now that they perhaps recognized a budding talent that was worth nurturing..."

One thing that needed no nurturing was her sense of fun: "One Harvest Festival I was in the choir, sitting beside a large window-sill, decorated with vegetables. I carefully selected a large potato and proceeded to pass it along the row. I think everyone was so surprised (it was in the middle of a sermon) that they just took it and passed it on. All went well until it reached the front row and was handed to a very devout lady, Gertrude Shackleton. She was so horrified that she just let it drop, and it fell almost at the feet of the preacher." He stared at it with much amazement and then turned to the choir, his eyes searching out the culprit and eventually fastening on Constance, with her head in her hands, shaking with laughter. She adds serenely, "They were good days in the choir, and I feel that they were the beginning of my musical appreciation."

MUSICAL DEVELOPMENT

Love of music was bred in Constance. Her mother was musical and had a good singing voice. However she had been one of four children to feed and clothe and there had never been any money for music lessons. With Constance, she decided, it should be different. "In the early days she struggled to pay one-and-ninepence for my piano lessons with a young man called Eric Pinkett, who insisted, if we did not turn up for any reason, that he must be paid." Unfortunately Constance had already learnt to play by ear and loved making up tunes, and did not enjoy the discipline required to master the piano. "I regret this very much, though I developed a very good ear and could sight-read anything, having been trained in the Tonic Sol-fa. I also had a very good memory, and still have to this day [1996], for which I am very thankful.

"It was not until later in my career when I went to the Royal Academy of Music that I was told that Tonic Sol-fa was old-fashioned and that I would have to learn the proper way of reading music. This completely unnerved me and really did affect my sight-reading. There is now a school of thought that we should go back to Tonic Sol-fa as it is easier to read and builds self-confidence. Vocally this was very noticeable at Covent Garden in the early days. Most of our tenors were from Wales. They had excellent voices, were good sight readers, and could scale a top C without difficulty. The trouble started when they had to read the music as printed and not in Tonic Sol-fa. They then began to think of high notes and low notes and their voices became much less secure."

If piano lessons were not a great success, churchgoing offered frequent opportunities for singing and acting, though it was not until Constance was seventeen that her true voice began to emerge. She still attended the little Methodist church in Bulwell and was a member of a young people's Guild, one of whose functions was to present an annual concert. On this occasion she sang Herbert Oliver's *Gypsy Spring*:

> Spring's a happy Gypsy, coming down the hills,
> Down the ways of April selling daffodils …

"When I stood up to sing I was so terrified that the first two words were hardly audible, but when it came to the word 'happy', the aspirate 'h' must have released all the breath tension and out came a huge sound that I had never heard before. I sang the whole song *treble forte* – I felt that if I once let go I would never find it again. Like my first broadcast it was an experience I shall never forget. I was hearing the sound as a composer hears sound, as though from another world, or as though a part of me was outside myself. It was then that people began to say, 'This girl has a voice. We must watch her.' After this, several musically-minded people from the church took me under their wing.

One of them, a lady who helped me to prepare a song, decided I should sing in a festival. She insisted on being called 'Madame' and was a rather buxom, jovial lady. When I went for my first lesson, almost her first remark was, 'Stand up straight my dear. Stick out Doris and Kate.' I was very embarrassed, having only just discovered that I *had* a Doris and Kate, and to this day I haven't found out which is Doris and which is Kate! But I love the story."

Thus began her experience of singing in competitive musical festivals which, as Constance remarks, was excellent training since the adjudicators were professional musicians and gave valuable advice. During this period she worked in an office as a book-keeper – a job she hated, though it taught her to add up columns of figures with great speed. "No calculators in those days, which I do not regret. We had to develop our own intelligence."

Her boss, Mr Young, was very kind. "I think he realized that office work was not my *forte* and would always allow me to take time off to enter the festivals. For my twenty-first birthday he gave me a beautiful music cabinet which I use and treasure to this day." However it was not until she began to win championship cups that it began to dawn on her that perhaps she had been given something very special.

She now began to take singing lessons with Roy Henderson, the well-known baritone, who lived in Nottingham. "I shall always be grateful to him for his wonderful help vocally and great generosity in the matter of fees. Officially a 'term' consisted of ten lessons but many times he extended this to twelve or more and not a word said. Thank you Roy for your understanding."

Her progress and development at this time can be measured by dates. In 1933 she joined the Nottingham Operatic Society and was quickly offered principal parts. In the same year she won the *Guardian* Silver Challenge Cup at the Nottingham Musical Festival. In 1935 she was the Nottingham Carnival Queen and in 1937 she made her first broadcast and passed her Grade 7 singing. The examiner's general assessment on this occasion hinted at her considerable potential:

> A charming voice. A most attractive style. Sings like an experienced singer and seems to take real pleasure in it. Should do extremely well. Bound to give pleasure wherever she sings. This is an exceptionally good candidate.

The broadcast was another milestone. She had been chosen to represent the Nottingham Operatic Society in a programme called *Songs from the Shows* and had to travel to Birmingham, which at that time was the only radio station for the Midlands. She was to sing Edward German's 'O Peaceful England' from *Merrie England* but before the song was transmitted she had to satisfy a casting panel. It was, she recalled, "quite a frightening experience."

"I was shown into a studio with no windows – very claustrophobic – and the casting panel of four were sitting in a box-like compartment at one end. It had a glass front looking into the studio, so I was able to see four faces peering at me. After I had sung, I was ushered into a small anteroom and told to wait. After about five minutes I heard this voice coming through singing 'O Peaceful England'. I had never heard my recorded voice before and it was quite unnerving. I felt there was another 'me' out there and that I was no longer on this earth. What a relief it was when Gwen Williams, who was one of the panel, came into the room and brought me back to earth by saying how much she had enjoyed my singing and was sure I would 'make it'. She remained a fan over the years and periodically I would receive a touching letter from her saying how much she had enjoyed my performance in this or that opera or concert."

She now began to attract wider attention. It was while she was playing the part of the Duchess in the Nottingham Operatic Society's production of *The Gondoliers* that she was spotted by the D'Oyly Carte opera company and pressed to audition with them:

"It was at the time that Bertha Lewis and Henry Lytton were famous names in the company and I felt that this was my big chance. Unfortunately my parents thought otherwise. The stage was not the place for a sensitive girl and I would never stand up to the hard life in the theatre. Besides, I had a good pensionable job as a book-keeper and I should think about the security. I had many sleepless nights thinking that this was my one great chance, and I had to choose between being a dutiful daughter or leaving home. Perhaps my parents were right and it was not a good idea. I did not take up the invitation but it caused me much distress at the time. Certainly if I had joined the D'Oyly Carte my life would have taken a very different turn. I continued studying with Roy Henderson and I began to be invited to sing in concerts and oratorios in local churches – mainly *The Messiah* and *Elijah*. I was immensely happy doing this and began to feel more and more that this was my work in life. But how? In those days there was no such thing as a student grant and if one's parents hadn't the money to finance one, there was only one other way: to try for a scholarship. As the urge began to grow stronger, I talked the problem over with Roy. By this time he too felt I should take the plunge and try for a scholarship at the Royal Academy of Music, where he had been a student." The Royal Academy of course meant education and qualifications – after all, when she left the Academy she could teach, couldn't she? Far better than a risky life in the theatre! Such seem to have been the thoughts of her parents. At any rate they raised no serious objection, and Constance accordingly presented herself for interview. The Principal of the Royal Academy at that time was Sir Stanley Marchant, and she sang for him and was interviewed by him. "He talked with me for a long time, asking many questions and wanting to know if this was really what I wanted to do. He felt that I had an outstanding gift but that it would entail a lot of hard, dedicated work if I came to the Academy." She must have convinced him of her determination for he awarded her the Tuer Scholarship for two years. This covered her tuition fees, but she still had to find the money to live in London. "I had saved up a little money from my concerts and, feeling that this was my real chance – now or never – I accepted." She was then 26 years old.

Constance had one last engagement to fulfil before going to London: she had been booked to give a recital at a church in West Bridgford on 4 September 1939 – but on 3 September Britain declared war on Germany. "I felt no-one would want to come to a concert at such a tragic time and so I cancelled the performance. What of my plans? The following Saturday I was due to go to London to begin my studies but everyone said I would be quite mad to go there in the circumstances: the capital would be the first place to be bombed. However I was convinced that it was right for me, and as the Academy was remaining open I felt that not even a war could stop me. I shall never forget the distress of my parents when we parted. I'm sure they thought they would never see me again."

---

1. Now Top Valley housing estate. Constance is commemorated in the name of one of the roads: Shacklock Close. The farmhouse, which was demolished to make way for some of the houses, was a T-shaped building with a 3-bay front and mullioned windows in the rear wing.

2. *The Prelude*, book I.

3. Albert Street School, Bulwell. I am grateful to Mrs Win Wilson of Aspley for confirming this since the early admissions registers for Albert Street School no longer exist. Mrs Wilson attended the same school and was a friend and contemporary of Constance's sister, Rosamund.

II

THE WAR YEARS

THE ACADEMY

In various ways fortune smiled on Constance during the next few years. The problem of where to live in London for example was solved for her before she ever got there.

During the mid-1930s she had saved whatever she could from her slender earnings in order to go on a cruise to the fjords of Norway. Perversely as it might seem, this was because she had always been afraid of water. "If I went on a cruise with no escape," she reasoned, "I would either be healed of the fear, or never go on water again – ever." The experiment worked, and she loved it. "Even one night when there was a storm, with thunder and lightning, I was not afraid and found myself standing on deck, looking out to sea and thinking what a wonderful sight it was. It looked just like a firework display. On another occasion, when there was a heavy swell and many people had to retire to their cabins with sea-sickness, I just had a terrible headache. I asked the ship's doctor if he could give me something to relieve it and he remarked, 'We are never sick but we too get bad heads. You must be a born sailor.' Little did he know."

On the final night of the cruise, at the big fancy-dress ball given by the captain, Constance went as Snow White and collected her Seven Dwarves from among the passengers. They won first prize. "Imagine my surprise and delight when, in 1996, one of the Dwarves – now a lady of ninety – wrote to me enclosing a snapshot of us all in our costumes. She said she had followed my career with great interest. It gave me so much joy to telephone her... What a lovely and happy surprise!"

It was during the cruise that Constance struck up a friendship with an artist lady, a painter. "She became very interested in my career and when, later, I wrote to her and told her that I was going to London to study, she most kindly offered me accommodation until I could get settled. I had £2 a week, eleven shillings of which went on rent, and the rest on food and other necessities. When I relate this to my students, I'm sure they think I came out of the Ark."

Life at the Academy was never going to be easy, given wartime conditions, but at least she had sympathetic tutors. Sir Stanley Marchant had arranged for her to study singing with Thomas Meukes, who had been Roy Henderson's teacher. She describes him as "a kindly man ... very down to earth. He seemed to understand all the problems of young students." As a case in point, she was down in the cloakroom one day when she heard herself being discussed by two fellow students in not very flattering terms. As it happened she was just then on her way to a lesson with Meukes and arrived feeling very depressed. She admits that she began the lesson "not singing very well."

'What is the matter, my dear?' Meukes enquired. 'What's on your mind?'

This of course was a difficult question for Constance, but Meukes persisted, refusing to continue the lesson until she had told him. When at length she explained, he replied:

'My dear girl, you should feel very happy. No-one talks about you in this place unless you are good.'

Confidence restored, she had an excellent lesson. Sadly, at the end of her first term, Meukes' health broke down and he had to retire from the Academy. Who was going to be her next teacher? She knew virtually nothing about the rest of the singing staff and was very worried. By this time she had become friendly with another student, Mildred Litherlow, who was studying accompaniment with Harold Craxten, the distinguished accompanist and teacher. Craxten had, on occasion, accompanied Dame Clara Butt, the famous contralto of the Edwardian era. Mildred explained Constance's problem to him and he invited Constance to come along to one of Mildred's lessons as a substitute singer. "I very much enjoyed the session and learnt a lot about the accompanist's approach to a song. Then he talked to me about a singing teacher, and I have never forgotten his words. 'Go to Frederick Austin. If he doesn't do you any good, he won't do you any harm.' " It was sound advice and Constance took it. She remained with Austin for the whole of her career until he died at the age of 80. "I'm told he was a wonderful Count in *The Marriage of Figaro*," she recalls. "He was tall and very good looking and it was easy to imagine him in the role. He was also an excellent musician and will be remembered for his arrangement of the music for John Gay's *The Beggar's Opera* and for composing the music for many films. He made a great difference to my life."

At the start of her second year life assumed a surreal quality for London was now in the throes of the Blitz. "When the siren went we fled down to the basement until the All Clear sounded. Looking back on those days I marvel that the Academy stayed open. I am very grateful that it did – my life would have taken a very different turn if it hadn't. When you are in the middle of a war you don't realize the great seriousness of it all." On more than one occasion Constance narrowly escaped death. "Once, I was on a bus, on my way to the Academy when the siren sounded. The bus continued, and not many minutes later the bus in front of us received a direct hit. On another occasion I was fire-watching from the house where I now lived in Belsize Road, which had six steps down to the pavement. The large block of flats opposite had been hit by incendiaries and was burning fiercely. The hose pipes had failed and the firemen were relying on buckets of water to control the blaze – an impossible task. I came out of the house carrying a large bucket of water – there were no lights of course – and as I hesitated on the top step to secure my footing a large piece of shrapnel just missed my nose. Had I not paused for that one second I too would have had a direct hit.

"The Italian couple who owned the house were very kind to the students staying there. We could practise for long hours and they never grumbled. In fact often we would find them sitting on the stairs listening to us. When the bombing got worse and the doodlebugs started to come over, they rented half a cottage in the country since they feared for the safety of their two children. One night the cottage was hit, killing one of their children and seriously injuring the other. Apart from a few minor mishaps their house in Belsize Road survived intact. One asked oneself many times: 'Why?' Looking back I realize how fortunate I was to come through it all unscathed because we had some terrible raids. I wonder now how I ever managed to study at such a time."

Occasionally there were lighter moments. One day, a block of flats opposite the Academy was badly bombed and the students helped in the rescue work. "The first victims to be rescued were an elderly lady of ninety and a parrot who was expressing himself very vehemently. We thought this very funny."

Another effect of the war was that the Academy was short of space. "Study rooms for practice were very difficult to find as they were all occupied by professors. There was one violin professor, Rousby Woofe, an excellent violinist and teacher but a rather eccentric and highly nervous man. I discovered that he didn't start teaching until 10.00 a.m., so I tried to arrive about 9.00 and borrow his room for practice. One morning however he came in early and glared through the glass door (he wore very thick-lensed glasses). When he entered the room I stood up immediately, a little surprised to see him.

His remarks were very gruff: 'Were you singing?'

'Well, I was trying to, Mr Woofe.'

'Good God. I thought it was a siren.' ".

At about this time, somebody organised First Aid classes at the Academy and Constance decided it would be wise to enrol. The course included demonstration lessons, and during one of these a male student was told to go to the back of the building and pretend that he had been wounded. He was to lie there until he was rescued. Unfortunately there was a good deal of turmoil going on in the building at the time and the demonstration was interrupted. When eventually Constance got around to rescuing him she found a note which read: 'Just died – gone home.'

With typical modesty, Constance makes no mention in her writings of her achievements at the RAM. Yet these were outstanding. In July 1941 she won the Sainton-Dolly Prize in singing and was awarded a scholarship and an exhibition which enabled her to continue at the Academy for a further three years. In 1942 she carried off more prizes and received the Academy Certificate of Merit. Finally, in the summer of 1943 she received the Parepa-Rosa Prize, the Gilbert R. Betjemann Memorial Prize, and the much-coveted Certificate of Merit with Distinction – the highest Annual Award of the Academy. She was now its most distinguished student vocalist.

Also there were concert appearances, now difficult to trace since the relevant programmes do not survive in the RAM archives. We know however, from what Constance herself said in the BBC radio interview already referred to that she sang the solo contralto part in an Academy performance of Debussy's *La Damoiselle elue*, conducted by Sir Henry Wood. Ten days after this performance, on the night of Saturday, 10 May 1941 the Queen's Hall was destroyed by enemy incendiary bombs. A concert by the London Philharmonic Orchestra, also under the baton of Sir Henry Wood, had been scheduled to take place there on the Sunday, and was hurriedly transferred to the main hall of the RAM. Partly as a way of thanking the Academy, and also because of her fine performance in the Debussy concert, Sir Henry invited Constance to sing 'Rule Britannia' as a defiant encore item at the end of the advertized programme. Subsequently of course she was to sing 'Rule Britannia' at the Last Night of the Proms on no less than ten occasions between 1950 and 1964.

WAR WORK

When Constance received the Academy Certificate of Merit with Distinction she still held a scholarship tenable until the end of July 1944. However she was now a post-graduate student and was being pursued by the Ministry of Labour.

It is difficult for those of us who live in a very different world to realize how war-time conditions effectively deprived people of their civil liberties. In 1941 every woman in Britain had to be registered, and those of working age who were without young children or not pursuing career qualifications were required to choose from a range of jobs considered helpful to the war effort. Many single women were drafted into the armed forces, where they functioned as auxiliaries on the 'Home Front'. For Constance, this would have meant a possibly catastrophic interruption to her burgeoning career. There was, however, one kind of war work – if she could win her way into it – in which she could put her musical talents to good use. This was CEMA: the Committee for the Encouragement of Music and the Arts, which had been taken under the wing of the Ministry of Labour to provide entertainment (and thus, it was hoped, to boost morale) in hospitals, factories and military camps across the UK. It was at this juncture that she received the following letter from the composer Granville Bantock:

Trinity College of Music

20 June 1943

Dear Miss Shacklock,

I hope that you will be able to undertake the Song Recital for the BBC London broadcast early in July, which was postponed from May 31, as it conflicted with my absence from London during the last three weeks. I saw Mr Arthur Wynn at the BBC before my departure, and arranged for the postponement.

It should be possible for you to obtain professional engagements with C.E.M.A, and I will speak to Sir Kenneth Barnes when I see him on Monday at the A.S.P.R.A. meeting, and I hope that an audition will be the prelude to a series of engagements.

I will expect you at 33 St George's Court for a rehearsal on Tuesday next at 12.0 noon.

With best wishes,

      Yours sincerely,

        Granville Bantock

Constance was duly engaged by CEMA and thus joined a select company of singers and instrumentalists, most of whom were already well known in the musical world. "It was," she says, "the best training I could possibly have had. I had to sing in factories and hospitals and also to the troops. I hated singing in the factories because I felt they really didn't want to hear us, and singing to the night-shift at 2.30 in the morning was my idea of purgatory. They had to give me strong black coffee to keep me awake.

"We usually worked as a team of three: a singer, an instrumentalist and an accompanist. My very first factory tour was with Redvers Llewellyn, the well-known Welsh baritone. He had a lovely voice and a delightful sense of humour and was a great character too. When I went out to sing my first two songs, all I could see were a few blank faces and four men playing cards just below the platform and eating thickly-cut sandwiches which they could hardly get into their mouths. They didn't seem the least bit interested in my singing and continued their game of cards. I came off stage feeling very deflated. Redvers saw my face and smiled, and said, 'Don't worry Luv. You'll get used to it.' I decided to watch and see how he reacted. During his first song I noticed him eyeing the card players and when he had finished he looked down at them and remarked, 'Why the hell didn't you trump that?' They looked up absolutely astonished. But they did listen to the rest of his songs.

"Singing to the troops was much more enjoyable and at times great fun. On one occasion I was told by the music adviser that one of his camp colleagues was an artist and had decorated the stage. He didn't warn me what the decorations were and when I walked on stage the expression on my face caused great laughter from the troops. All around were figures of nude ladies sitting in very provocative positions on the knees of high-ranking uniformed officers. After the initial shock I managed to collect myself and sing my songs which, I'm happy to say, were very much appreciated. The troops were usually very good audiences.

"On another occasion I was singing at an American camp in the South of England. One of my songs was Frank Bridges' 'Love went a-riding.' After I had hit the top F# at a very dramatic climax there was some consternation at the back of the hangar where the concert was being held. I thought that perhaps someone had fainted. At the end of the concert (which I had shared with a violinist) I was told what had happened. Behind the chairs set out for the audience was a long trestle table where the boys wrote their letters. On it had been a large chunky glass inkwell which my top note had smashed into tiny fragments like a windscreen. The Colonel jokingly said afterwards that he would not ask me to sing if there were any valuable chandeliers around. The only other time this happened to me was at Covent Garden. When I was singing an aria, one of the overhead arc lamps smashed, but I kept quiet about this, suspecting that I was the guilty one. It gave me a lot of food for thought as to why, when troops were crossing bridges, they had to break step, and why, in one of the bible stories, when the trumpeters blew loudly, the walls of Jericho fell down. Sound has some very peculiar properties.

"On another occasion at a camp in the South of England, I had just started to sing my first song when the door at the back of the hall opened and in came three wounded boys on crutches. I waited for them to get seated and then continued. After the concert I spoke to them. That very morning they had been fighting on the Normandy beaches, and after being wounded they had been treated in a local hospital and then flown back to England. They just couldn't believe that they were back home and listening to a concert.

"I always enjoyed singing to the troops – they seemed to appreciate our concerts very much. I'm sure it was a pleasant break from their rigid training, both physical and mental. I always tried to dress attractively as I believe this is part of a singer's training: to express beauty not only in the voice but in one's appearance too. Quite often I got a few wolf whistles, but I always felt that this was a compliment and returned their exuberance with a big smile.

"I was surprised to find how many of the troops loved the opera. One of the boys told me that when they were stationed in Italy they went to the opera out of sheer boredom thinking, 'At least we'll have a good laugh,' but had been completely won over and couldn't wait to hear more. What a lovely introduction.

"Singing in hospitals I found deeply disturbing. On one occasion, at the famous hospital at East Grinstead where all the special plastic surgery was done, I was waiting outside the ward for my cue to go in and sing when a tall boy came and stood beside me. I looked at him and thought I was going to faint. His whole head was swathed in bandages: the result of an injury sustained while driving a tank. I was told that they could give him a new face but that he would never see again. He was American, just 25 years old, and had been married just three weeks before coming to Europe. I found myself wondering what his young bride's reaction would be when he returned home. Would she have the courage to face up to the terrible tragedy and help him, or would it break up their lives together? I couldn't get him out of my mind and I kept on thinking how evil war is.... Singing to the troops and in hospitals was something I shall never forget. I learnt so much about life and what its true values are.

BALLET INTERLUDE

"The war was now coming to an end and I began to wonder what I would be doing next. One day my singing teacher, Frederick Austin, rang me and told me that the International Ballet was planning to produce Milton's masque *Comus* at the London Coliseum. A friend and colleague of his, Ernest Irving, was conducting and would I be interested to go along and sing for him and the Inglebys who were the Directors? (Their daughter Mona was the principal dancer). The salary was £25 a week. I was very excited. The part was the goddess Sabrina. There was one lovely solo and a duet. I duly went along and sang to them and was offered the role. I thought I would be tucked away in the pit to sing my part but when I was summoned to go for a dress fitting it suddenly dawned on me that I was to be on stage with the ballet dancers. I, a farmer's daughter, used to playing cricket with the neighbouring farmer's four boys and climbing trees, doing ballet! I must admit, at first the thought terrified me, but it was such a beautiful role to perform. I knew I must overcome my fears, work to get inside the role and portray her as the beautiful character she was. I went to the ballet rehearsals, watched the graceful movements of the dancers, and then went home and practised them. I soon became intrigued and fascinated by movement and how one can express thoughts in bodily action. It was a wonderful experience, and how deeply grateful I am for the privilege of working with that dedicated company for my first professional engagement. It gave me hope for the future."

As Sabrina in Milton's *Comus*, September 1945

III

LET'S MAKE AN OPERA COMPANY

One day, while Constance was still with the International Ballet, she had another telephone call from Frederick Austin. He told her that a new opera company was being formed at Covent Garden and that she should apply for an audition – which she did. It was to be the turning point of her career.

Understandably that first audition was something of an ordeal. "Singing on the Covent Garden stage for the first time was awe-inspiring: the vastness of the auditorium and the fact that it could mean so much to my career made me feel very nervous. Despite this I felt I sang well, but when I heard nothing for many months I resigned myself to having failed. Then another letter came, inviting me for a second audition – and then for a third, and a fourth…"

Miraculously as it seemed to Constance, she was then invited to join the company – and on a principal's salary, not just as a member of the chorus. "I felt I was dreaming and would suddenly wake up."

The circumstances surrounding the formation of the new company were complex and – it seemed to many at the time – idealistic. Before the Second World War the Royal Opera House had been a purely commercial undertaking:

seasons of opera and ballet alternating with film shows, lectures, cabaret, and the occasional use of the building as a dance hall. With the outbreak of hostilities however, opera and ballet productions ceased, and the theatre was leased to Mecca Cafes for a period of five years as a *palais de danse*. When the lease came up for renewal in December 1944 the end of the war was already in sight. The owners of the theatre, Covent Garden Properties Ltd., preferred to see the building revert to its pre-war role and agreed to transfer the lease to the music publishers Boosey and Hawkes, who were wanting to venture into live opera on their own account. Mecca, for whom the theatre had been a small gold-mine, were dismayed when they saw themselves being elbowed out. They argued that since Boosey and Hawkes had no experience of running an opera house their bid was invalid, and they threatened legal action. The problem was resolved when Boosey and Hawkes appealed to CEMA, the government funded Committee for the Encouragement of Music and the Arts, precurser of the Arts Council. With CEMA's support, and the promise of an ongoing subsidy from the Treasury, Covent Garden became in effect a state-run concern, its object being the creation of a National Opera Company. In this way the theatre was secured as a permanent home for opera and ballet, though as regards opera, it meant starting again entirely from scratch.

The problems were enormous. The newly-appointed Musical Director, Karl Rankl, had to assemble an orchestra and an opera company on the basis of individual applications, and he had just six months in which to do it.

Around two thousand singers were auditioned, 'among them postal clerks, milkmen, housewives and farm hands. Few had ever sung for money or could read a score.... Rankl could take nothing for granted; he had to teach them the art from scales up'. [1]

There was a fairy-tale quality about the whole undertaking, and the musical world was understandably sceptical. By professional standards the pay was derisory: eight pounds a week for chorus singers, and forty for principals; yet to most of the successful applicants it was the realization of an improbable dream ('I thought I was a millionairess,' said Constance.)[2] Operas were to be sung in English to encourage a wider clientele, and the relatively modest overheads (modest in terms of opera that is) were reflected in the price of tickets. A seat in the gallery was only half-a-crown (12½p) and for thirteen shillings and sixpence (two-thirds of a pound) you could have a place in the front stalls. (Compare these prices with the £150 charged for quite indifferent seats after the reopening in 2000.) This was democracy at its most venturesome, and it was matched by a camaraderie and dedication among the staff that was perhaps unique in the annals of grand opera:

> Only at Covent Garden would you find dancers rehearsing on stage at four in the morning, no other slot being available. Nowhere else did wage clerks stay on past midnight to proofread a report from another department that had to reach the Arts Council by morning. Here alone did stage hands knowingly risk and, on tragic

occasion, sacrifice their lives on machinery that was defunct before the First World War and still in use decades later. Only at Covent Garden would the doorman look after the dogs of two dancers who were going on holiday, while the nonagenarian ballet-founder, Dame Ninette de Valois, stood in a queue for a cup of canteen tea, shunning special treatment. In no other opera house would a music director, a knight of the realm, take a broom and sweep the pit floor before rehearsal, taking care not to knock down the table on which Puccini had stood during rehearsals for the first *Bohème*. [3]

To begin with of course, the company was inexperienced and inadequate: their singers needed time to develop, to master the different styles of singing and to acquire confidence. Yet the raw material was there in abundance. ' "You have the finest collection of voices in the world," Rankl told the new Chorus Master. "It is up to you to make them into a chorus" '. [4]

The real problem was in bringing forward new principals. It had always been taken for granted that English voices, though excellent for oratorio, lacked richness, power and dramatic depth. They might do well enough in small opera houses like Glyndebourne but were thought to be incapable of producing the big effects required in vast auditoria like La Scala and Covent Garden. The dogma had been repeated to the point where it was accepted as a solemn truth, and it generated what Montague Haltrecht called 'second place mentality'.[5] British opera singers were there 'merely to provide a backing to show off distinguished foreigners'. [6]

If this kind of thing meant little to the new company (most of whom were living on cloud nine) it meant a good deal to the musical press, which for the most part refused to believe in the possibility of high quality English opera. Covent Garden productions came in for a barrage of criticism, much of which seems in retrospect to have been heavy-handed and unfair. It was not that there was no room for improvement – clearly there was, and clearly foreign guest singers were going to be necessary both to strengthen the company and to teach by example. Rather it was that the press demanded standards which, to start with, were just not attainable. In these circumstances, Constance's gradual rise to stardom was to prove all the more remarkable.

*

Training and rehearsals began in September 1946 ("I'm sure I was the first person to enter the stage door on that first morning," Constance later confessed) and the company were given three months to prepare for their debut. Wisely it was decided to commence with a hybrid work, Purcell's *The Fairy Queen*, derived from Shakespeare's *A Midsummer Night's Dream*. It involved a cast of straight actors, sections of the Covent Garden Ballet (including Fonteyn and Moira Shearer) and a small group of principal singers (Audrey Bowman, Muriel Burnett, Gladys Palmer,

Constance Shacklock, Bruce Dargavel, Edgar Evans and David Franklin) in what were really supporting roles. *The Fairy Queen* opened on 12 December 1946, ran for 24 nights and was adjudged moderately successful. Not so the company's first forays into grand opera. *Carmen*, which opened on 14 January 1947, was described by Philip Hope Wallace in *The Guardian* as 'a dire penance', and a headline in the *Evening News* protested: 'This British *Carmen* Is All Wrong.' Singing such a passionate opera in English was felt not to help. *Carmen* was followed by Massenet's *Manon*, and then by *The Magic Flute* and *Rosenkavalier*, none of which impressed the critics. Flaws in production came in for particularly heavy criticism from the immensely influential Ernest Newman, who protested that 'only taste of the worst kind could have made possible some of the inanities and vulgarities plastered on a performance of *The Magic Flute* ... and which made a great deal of the *Rosenkavalier* production so depressing an experience for those of us with memories of Covent Garden in its great days. The acting in general,' he thought, 'was the worst feature' of *Rosenkavalier* and he conceded that 'there was not a vast amount of fault to find with much of the singing considered as such.' If this was damning with faint praise he had one word of real encouragement:

> I was much taken with the Annina of Constance Shacklock, whom I cannot remember having seen or heard before. This young lady sings very well, moves with an ease and grace that are a joy to the spirit no less than to the eye, and appears to have the makings of an operatic actress in her

> – though like most of the rest of the company she is inclined to use a pot of paint for an effect where a brushful would suffice. – *Sunday Times*, 27 April 1947

Annina is, of course, a minor role, and the minor roles in *Rosenkavalier* do rather invite grotesqueries and 'pots of paint'. In any case Constance was grateful to Newman and always considered that it was this review which led to her rapid promotion within the company.

An opportunity to show what she could do came during a close-season tour of the provinces (August– October 1947) in which Constance replaced Edith Coates as Carmen. The provinces were duly impressed and for once the press notices glowed:

> The Covent Garden Opera Company gave a satisfying matinee performance of *Carmen* on Saturday. Constance Shacklock's portrayal was a splendid study of Carmen's sweet and turbulent moods... (*Liverpool Evening Express,* 6 September)

> The Covent Garden Company completed their Manchester repertoire at the Opera House on Saturday with Bizet's *Carmen*. The performance was dominated by the superb Carmen of Constance Shacklock, who possesses the physical grace, intense personality and the rich voice demanded by the role. (*Daily Telegraph,* 22 September)

Say, if you will, that the provinces are more easily satisfied than London. It was, nevertheless, a promising debut, and thereafter she was the automatic choice for the part of Carmen, over the years singing it on no less than 110 occasions.

And accolades were what Covent Garden desperately needed. Realizing that the Royal Opera House could not afford another London season like the last one, the General Administrator, David Webster, was busy adjusting his plans. Distinguished foreign principals would have to be brought in, and he was anxious to secure *Peter Grimes* for the Garden, following its sensational premiere at Sadler's Wells. Negotiations were tricky, for Britten preferred small-scale opera and had his own English Opera Group. Nevertheless he was tempted by an offer to write a large opera for Covent Garden, and agreed to Webster's plans for a revival of *Grimes* when he was assured that the original principals, Joan Cross and Peter Pears, would be invited to lead the new cast. *Grimes* duly opened on 6 November 1947 with Constance in the role of Mrs Sedley.

"This," she conceded, "was a real challenge – the village scandal-monger. I had a grey corkscrew curl wig; my nose was made up to look long and pointed, and I wore a pair of hideous steel-rimmed glasses. I had to walk as though I had rheumatism and change my voice to fit with the character. [This caused the *New Statesman* to protest that 'it was a gross and painful error to have instructed (or allowed) Constance Shacklock, as Mrs Sedley, to *croak* her entire part, as though she were the Witch in *Hansel and Gretel*']. I looked so awful that in my pride I refused to have my photograph taken – something which I now very much regret. However one special evening stands out in my memory. Following one of the performances, a party was given for Benjamin Britten to congratulate him... We were honoured to have with us as guests that evening the Prince and Princess Collona of Luxemburg, and when I was presented to the Prince in the crush bar he asked if I'd enjoyed the performance. 'Yes,' I replied, 'but it was a real challenge to interpret the role of Mrs Sedley.' 'Mrs Sedley!' the Prince repeated incredulously. 'I just don't believe it!' – and he called to his wife, who was talking to David Webster: 'Come here, my dear. This is unbelievable. This lady says she played the role of Mrs Sedley.' They both stared at me in disbelief and it took David Webster quite a while to convince them that I was the same person. I must admit I looked very different in my evening dress and regalia!"

The other big event of the 1947-48 Season was the visit of the great Norwegian soprano Kirsten Flagstad to sing in *Tristan und Isolde*. By that time, Flagstad was nearing the end of her career but her voice was still thrilling and her reputation so enormous that the whole company regarded her with trepidation – none more so than Constance, who had been selected to sing Brangäne. "I remember at one of the early rehearsals we were working in the crush bar. It was the second act of *Tristan*, when Brangäne gives Isolde the love potion from a casket. I was so much in awe of her that I was almost afraid to go near her. She whispered very gently, 'You can touch me, my dear, I'm real!'" It was, as somebody said on a different occasion, the start of a beautiful friendship.

"What I loved about Flagstad was that she never made me feel a little secondary artist," said Constance, who soon became her constant companion. "She embraced me in her great artistry and love, so that in three months I didn't recognize myself. Not only had my voice developed beyond recognition but I had changed as a person. I became immeasurably more confident and realized that if I worked sincerely and with dedication I could fulfil what I felt was my life's work. It was Flagstad who gave me the inspiration."

Another thing which would help to explain the extraordinary rapport which developed between the two women is that they had both suffered cruelly from the effects of war: Constance through her father, and Flagstad through the fate of her husband. After the liberation of Norway he had been accused of collaborating with the Germans – on what grounds, we don't know: the King of Norway always maintained he was innocent – and he died in prison while awaiting trial. Constance was a lifelong pacifist.

At any rate Flagstad became her model. "I recall another occasion. She had developed a very bad chest and could hardly speak, let alone sing. David Webster searched the world for a replacement but no-one was available. In the circumstances Flagstad agreed – as she said – 'to have a go.' Webster went on stage and explained matters to the audience, adding that Mme Flagstad was prepared to go on and try to sing the role but that if her voice did not hold the performance would have to be cancelled. Were the audience prepared to accept this? There was an overwhelming 'Yes!' So the orchestra started. I shall never forget that performance. Just before the curtain went up she whispered, 'Think of me, dear.' For the first fifteen minutes her voice was about a quarter of its normal strength but I could see that she was concentrating on her deep breathing to take away the congestion and strain from her throat. By the end of the first act her voice was nearly back to normal and at the end of the performance the audience gave her a standing ovation. From then on, whenever I had a little snuffle or sore throat, I didn't panic but thought of Flagstad, and I believe that in the whole of my career I only had to cancel six performances for illness.

"On another occasion, at Flagstad's 120th performance of Isolde at the Garden, she had a slight memory lapse for about ten bars. Eric [Constance's husband – see below] was in the prompt box that night and he just very quietly continued singing her line until she picked it up again. I doubt if anyone in the theatre was aware of this. Her remark later was, 'I just had a blank-out. We are all human, dear, and a big thank you to Eric.' Another great lesson: put failure behind you.

"I once asked her why she did not teach, as she had so much to give. Her reply surprised me. 'I wouldn't know how. I know exactly where I put a top G: I know what it feels like, but I couldn't tell *you* where to put it. We are all made physically different…..' "

It was Constance's Brangäne that really put her on the musical map. For once, the critics were almost unanimous in acknowledging the emergence of a top-rank English singer. Of course there were plenty of superlatives for Flagstad, and at this distance of time it is good to be reminded what a voice she had:

> There is no doubt that Kirsten Flagstad is one of the greatest artists of our time. That vast voice soars along, pure and round in tone from end to end, without a touch of hardness above or hoarseness below to mar its amazing leaps, as clear and mellow in its powerful *fortes* as it is caressing in its *pianissimos*. (*Sound*, May 1948)

But the same reviewer continued:

> A most important factor in a successful production of this opera is the quality of its Brangäne. In Constance Shacklock we had a fine one, a Brangäne who to an unearthly and wild beauty added a fine voice and an inspired acting ability.

Ernest Newman was equally impressed:

> Constance Shacklock sang the exacting Brangäne music excellently; she seems to have the makings of a first rate Wagnerian singer in

her. (*The Sunday Times*, 22 February 1948)

Another notable critic, Arthur Jacobs, had no doubts on this score:

> Flagstad and Hotter gave triumphant performances. No-one expected anything else from them. More noteworthy – though hardly surprising in view of her past work – is the emergence as a true Wagner star of Constance Shacklock, who plays a most convincing Brangäne. (*The Tribune*, 12 March 1948)

Some other reviewers were, if anything, more emphatic:

> Constance Shacklock displayed a volume, and at times a quality, of voice which which made her a not unworthy confidante of Mme Flagstad. (Martin Cooper in the *Spectator*, 27 February 1948)

> Constance Shacklock (as Isolde's handmaid) produces both tone and volume which rival her mistress's (*What's on in London*, 27 February 1948)

And so on and so on, with scarcely a dissenting voice. Appropriately and delightfully there survives among Constance's papers a telegram sent to her just before she went on stage for the first time as Brangäne:

BEST WISHES FOR A HUGE SUCCESS IN YOUR MOST IMPORTANT ROLE SO FAR = DAVID WEBSTER.

For very different reasons too the role of Brangäne was to bring joy to Constance and alter her life. In deference to the foreign guest singers, it had been decided to break the house rule and sing the opera in the original German. Constance had very little knowledge of German, and when she was allotted the part of Brangäne in the early summer of 1947, she sought the help of Eric Mitchell, the company's organist, assistant chorus master and repetiteur, who spoke German with an easy proficiency. He coached her, fell in love with her, and within a matter of weeks they were married. It was the beginning of a notable musical partnership and of many years of happiness. Thereafter, Eric was almost invariably her accompanist when she gave recitals.

Curiously the honeymoon was actually planned as something quite different. "I had become very friendly with Doris Doree, an American singer on contract to the Garden, and we had decided to go on holiday together to Lucerne. One day, during a coffee break between coaching sessions with Eric, we talked of holidays in Switzerland. When I told him that Doris and I were planning to go to Lucerne he said it was a place he had always wished to visit and asked whether he could come along with us. He promised he would carry our bags. After discussing it with Doris we had a good laugh that he should want to come with two females, but why not – especially as he would

Eric and Constance: Just Married

carry our bags?!! So I wrote to the hotel and asked for another room for our repetiteur friend. It was only later – about six weeks before the holiday – that Eric proposed to me during a rehearsal break. We then had to write to the hotel and tell them our news. They were delighted and gave us a lovely suite overlooking the lake. Dear Doris graciously disappeared out of the picture."

To return to the season 1947-48. Three months before the arrival of Flagstad, and at very short notice, Constance deputized for the indisposed Edith Coates as the gypsy Azucena in *Il Trovatore* and again scored 'a personal triumph' (*The Star*, 18 November 1947). She also sang Marina in *Boris Godunov* ('looks, glamour, and lovely tone' – *The Tribune*, 21 May 1948), Magdalene in *The Mastersingers*, and Grimgerda in *The Valkyrie*. 1948 also marked her emergence as a regular performer on the concert platform and with the BBC. It was a measure of her growing reputation that in July 1948 she was invited to sing the solo contralto part in Mozart's *Requiem* under the baton of Sir Thomas Beecham. What lent particular sweetness to the occasion was that Beecham, then fretting at his current exclusion from Covent Garden, where he had conducted before the war, viewed the present Company with ill-disguised hostility and lost no opportunity to deplore its musical standards. Other highlights included two nights at the Buxton Festival, where she shared the honours with the celebrated oboist Leon Goosens; and two appearances at the Proms. There is a magic moment in the career of any major performer which may be likened to a crossing of the Equator, when the language of reviewers undergoes a

As Azucena in *Il Trovatore* (photo: Houston Rogers)

subtle change. An artist ceases to be just 'promising' or 'a discovery', and becomes instead an accepted part of the musical scene. Constance had now definitely crossed her Equator.

---

1. ©Norman Lebrecht, 2007, *Covent Garden: The Untold Story*, pp.67-8 first published by Simon & Schuster UK Ltd. A CBS Company.

2. *ibid*, p.68

3. *ibid*, p.7.

4. Montague Haltrecht, *The Quiet Showman: Sir David Webster and the Royal Opera House*, Collins 1975, p.83.

5. *ibid*, p.83.

6. *ibid*, p.86

IV

ENTER THE MAESTRO

At the end of the first season at Covent Garden, Constance had been asked by Karl Ranki to understudy the title roles of Carmen and Octavian (*Der Rosenkavalier*), together with Amneris in *Aida* and Azucena in *Il Trovatore* – all major roles for the mezzo. She learnt – or partly learnt – the role of Carmen during her honeymoon in Switzerland. Eric obligingly rowed her out into the middle of Lake Lucerne where she could practise, and he could coach her, in seclusion. In fact she was soon singing all four roles on a regular basis.

In *Der Rosenkavalier* she graduated to the role of Octavian on the second night of the 1948-49 season, and in the words of one reviewer, 'whatever the merits of the rest of the cast, it was Constance Shacklock in the role of Octavian... who deserves the highest praise. Her realization of this very difficult role was a triumph, and among the greatest things I have seen on the Covent Garden or any other operatic stage' *(Musical Express*, 5 November 1948). She was to refine and develop her Octavian over several years. In fact it took Rankl's successor Erich Kleiber to bring the very best out of her (and to transform the orchestra and the entire company), but those first performances were sufficient to establish her as the house Octavian for as long as she remained at Covent Garden, and indeed almost to the end of her operatic career.

Much has been written about Karl Rankl, the company's first musical director. He was never popular with the critics, nor for that matter with Covent Garden audiences, partly because he was not a great name but mainly because of his nervous temperament: 'ever busy, ever anxious. He makes his way through bush and briar, hacking if need be' (*Musical Times*, December 1948). He is said to have been a humourless disciplinarian and he never had the ability to sit back, enjoy a performance and let the orchestra 'sing'. Yet it was Rankl who did the spade work, creating both orchestra and chorus out of virtually nothing. It is a measure of his achievement that what was lacking in his own handling of the Garden's musical resources could be supplied by Kleiber and Beecham with a few deft touches; and after their guest appearances the orchestra continued to play sensitively and sweetly for Rankl himself. Sadly by this time he was almost out of contract. He departed, unmourned by most, at the end of July 1951.

Constance's portrait of Rankl is more or less what one might expect, though she tempers it with sympathy, and a very real sense of what was owing to him. "Rankl .... was a very dedicated musician and did so much for Covent Garden in the early days. We were all very much afraid of him: he was such a disciplinarian, and yet for his tight rein I shall always be grateful. If for any reason we were one or two minutes late we dreaded facing him because he could be very sarcastic. He used to say, 'If the rehearsal is at ten o'clock, I want you on stage ready to start; not just walking through the stage door.' The punctuality which he instilled has always remained with me and I'm usually well in advance of time if I have an appointment. He was a very highly strung little man. Maybe the war years had left their mark on him, and also he realized, I think, the enormity of the task he had taken on as Musical Director of the new company. He valued very much the help of a fellow countryman, Peter Gelhorn, a fine musician and conductor, who was at his side at most of the rehearsals. I remember that on one occasion, a cleaner started hoovering in the foyer but could be very clearly heard in the theatre. Rankl turned to Peter and said, 'Gelhorn, for heaven's sake stop that woman. Hoovers and Howes give me the nerves.' (Howes was the music critic of *The Times* and unfortunately not very gracious in some of his remarks about Rankl's performances). It sounded so funny in his German accent.

"Actually the orchestra was very fond of Rankl and occasionally enjoyed pulling his leg. Once, on April 1st, we were about to rehearse the first act of *Tristan*. In his usual way he ran onto the rostrum and started conducting. The orchestra started to play the Overture to *Carmen* with great gusto. I thought Rankl would fall off the rostrum with horror.

" 'Gentlemen, vot are you doing? This is a rehearsal for *Tristan*, not *Carmen*.

"All of us by this time could hardly control our laughter, whereupon Joseph Shadwick, the Leader, said, 'Sorry

Maestro, it's April Fool's Day.' Rankl looked rather blank and during the coffee break he turned to Peter Gelhorn and said, 'Gelhorn, vot is April Fool's Day?' I don't know what explanation Peter gave him but we all very much enjoyed the joke.

"One of the operas he loathed conducting was Richard Strauss's *Salome*: not for the music but for the production and outlandish costumes and scenery by Salvador Dali. It really did cause an uproar with both the company and the audiences, when it was first staged in 1949. Some of the costumes were almost impossible to wear. I describe my head-gear for Herodias as a boat and a blancmange with a tree on top because that is what it looked like. It completely covered my ears and came down to my shoulders. Eventually I managed to persuade the designer that I must have my ears free from the drapery, otherwise I could not hear. Ljuba Welitsch, who sang Salome, refused to wear the costume designed for her. The original idea was a caterpillar casting off its skins in the dance of the seven veils. After a lot of very heated discussion it ended with Salome casting off a flimsy drape each time – not quite what Dali had envisaged, but it didn't seem to spoil the production. Welitsch and the rest of us found it very exciting to get the reactions of the audience. Peter Brook was the producer, but he and Rankl were certainly not in harmony in any way!!

"Ljuba Welitsch was one of the finest Salomes I've ever seen and worked with. She scaled this difficult role vocally with such ease and control and had the right temperament too. She was a very strong character. Working with her in *Aida* was another revelation. Jimmy Johnston, one of our leading tenors at the Garden, had sung with her in *Tosca*. In the torture scene, when Cavaradossi is literally thrown out of the torture chamber onto the stage in front of Tosca, she goes to him and envelops him in her arms. Jimmy's comment to Eric was, 'My God, she's tough. She nearly strangled me with her passion. Tell Constance to watch out in *Aida*!' Eric's reply was, 'I'm sure Constance will cope.'

In the second act there's a very dramatic scene between the slave girl Aida and the princess Amneris, who discovers that Aida and Radames, the leader of the triumphant Egyptian army, are in love. Unfortunately Amneris is in love with him too. When she discovers what is going on from Aida's own lips, in her passion she throws Aida to the ground. At the first performance Ljuba got hold of me first and held my wrists like a vice. Having been warned by Jimmy of her great strength, I put all my own strength into my next move and sent her flying across the stage. Thank goodness she went sideways and not forwards, otherwise she would have landed in the orchestra pit. My first thought was, 'She'll strangle me when we get off stage.' Imagine my surprise when she threw her arms around me and said, 'You are my friend. I like you. You have temperament.' From then on, our performances were electrifying!"

It was during the 1948-49 season that Constance began to emerge as a prominent figure on the concert platform and with the BBC. She sang Martha in a concert performance of Gounod's *Faust* and took part in the Christmas *Messiah* in Durham Cathedral; in a BBC broadcast of Stanford's *Stabat Mater* and in two performances of the Verdi *Requiem* at the Albert Hall, one of which was also broadcast. There were also numerous recitals, including an appearance at Leeds with Luigi Infantino, the celebrated tenor from La Scala. If this was all grist to the mill and made her more widely known (she was the subject of a major article in *Picture Post* on 20 November 1948), it also hinted at future problems. Over the next few years she expanded her repertoire to include Bach's *Mass in B Minor* and the *St John Passion*, Handel's *Solomon* and *Israel in Egypt*, Beethoven's *Choral Symphony*, the *Missa Solemnis* and the Mass in D, Mendlessohn's *Elijah*, Brahms' *Alto Rhapsody*, Dvorak's *Stabat Mater*, Elgar's *Sea Pictures*, *The Music Makers*, *Gerontius* and *The Kingdom*, Mahler's *Das Lied von der Erde*, concert versions of several operas, and various lesser known works. Yet versatility was bought at a price. Thereafter, apart from taking the lead part in four performances of Britten's *Gloriana* in 1953, and a single appearance as Cherubino in *The Marriage of Figaro*, she undertook no new major operatic roles, although she continued as a regular House choice in the roles of Carmen, Brangäne and Amneris. Her divided interests were a factor – though not the most important one – in a career crisis which belongs to a later chapter and which deprived her of international opera engagements at a time when she keenly desired them. For the time being however, everything seemed to be going her way, although success was about to cost her an acutely embarrassing incident. One day in 1948 the telephone rang in the Mitchell's studio flat in South Kensington, and Constance picked up the receiver. A voice said, 'This is Erich Kleiber, and I want to hear you sing.'

'Who?' asked Constance, not recognizing the name.

'Erich Kleiber, and I would like to hear you sing.'

"I said I would be very happy to come and sing for him but he replied that he liked to see artists actually performing. I told him that I was singing Magdalena in *Die Meistersinger* at the Garden that night but it was completely sold out and there was no chance of his getting a seat. His reply was, 'I think I can manage that!'

"My husband Eric was standing nearby and I could see his face getting redder and redder. When I finally put down the receiver, he said, 'Do you realize you were talking to one of the world's greatest conductors?' My heart sank. Had I thrown away a golden opportunity? Kleiber subsequently became a wonderful friend to me and never referred to the telephone conversation, although I'm sure he had many good laughs about it. One day at a rehearsal he remarked, 'I have to like my singers to work with them. You cannot make music together if there is any disharmony.' What words of wisdom."

Kleiber's interest in Constance had reference to a forthcoming Festival of the Dutch Wagner Society at which he was to be the guest conductor, and it resulted in her being asked to sing, along with Flagstad and Hans Hotter, in four performances of *Tristan and Isolde* in

Amsterdam and at The Hague – an honour never before conferred on a British artist. She recalls that after the first performance in Amsterdam there was a large reception. "I was sitting next to the Festival Director and at one point I saw him staring across the table with a very pensive look in his eyes. I said to him, 'A penny for them.' He whispered in reply, 'If anyone had told me two years ago that I would be sitting and eating with Germans, I would have said, "Never!" At that time we were eating the tulip bulbs out of the fields to keep us alive.' Then he looked down at the delicious food which had been prepared for us, gave me a sad smile, and said, 'Only music could have brought us together.'"

She also recalls being driven by their very kind agent from Amsterdam to The Hague. "Suddenly the agent exclaimed, 'There's Queen Wilhelmina!' Looking out of the car I expected to see a coach and horses. In fact there was the Queen pedalling away on her bicycle. Our agent told us that she did it every day as her exercise [she was then in her 69th year]. Knowing how carefully our own Royal Family are guarded I really felt he was pulling my leg and it took a lot of persuasion to convince me that it really was the Queen. The agent had a very charming wife and a four-and-a-half year old daughter who spoke to the Germans in German and then to me in perfect English. It made me very conscious of my own language shortcomings."

To come back to Kleiber. David Webster wanted him as Rankl's successor but at that stage of his career he was unwilling to tie himself down with long-term engagements.

What he was prepared to offer was a series of short 'seasons' as a guest conductor, and with this, Webster had to be content. It was enough to raise the profile of Covent Garden and to give the critics something to get excited about. His first appearances were in the winter of 1950-51 when Rankl was still in the House. He returned for a similar period the following winter, briefly in May 1952, and for a final spell in the spring and early summer of 1953. During all this time the Opera House was without a permanent Musical Director – a situation which was not without its advantages since it enabled Webster to bring in other famous names: Clemens Krauss, Rudolph Kempe and Barbirolli among them.

It would be wrong however to think of Kleiber as just another visiting conductor. His influence pervaded the House: he bonded with the orchestra and the singers and he let it be known that, in his opinion, British artists were second to none. He is even reported to have said that if he could have packed up Covent Garden and got it into his suitcase he would have taken it with him wherever he went. His involvement with the Royal Opera House is illustrated by his performance there, in May 1952, of Beethoven's *Choral Symphony*, as a first step to creating a benevolent fund for its players and singers. Constance remembered him with profound affection:

"[On his first visit] Kleiber was with us for about three months and the standard of the company rose beyond recognition. He was not only a great conductor but a great psychologist. He gave all of us the confidence to express our gifts. He was the singers' dream conductor. Mentally he sang every note with us and each performance was a deep experience.

"We all loved him, not only as a conductor but as a person. Many of the stories about him show what a really loving, understanding person he was. During a rehearsal of *Der Rosenkavalier*, one of our Welsh singers, Ryland Davies, playing the part of the Attorney, seemed to be having some difficulty with the music. Kleiber asked him if he had thought why Strauss had written so many rests during one phrase: 'May it – please – your Lordship,' etc. Rudd, as he was affectionately called, didn't know. Kleiber then told him that the Attorney was an asthmatic old boy and that the rests were written for him to gasp out his breath. Rudd tried to sing it that way and nearly choked himself. The rest of us laughed loudly. Rudd said, 'Sorry Sir. I can't do it.'

" 'Of course you can, my boy. You're an artist.'

"There was dead silence from all of us. Rudd made the most wonderful character out of the Attorney and from then on he seemed to bloom in every way. Kleiber had this effect on all of us.

"Another time, we were rehearsing the second act of *Der Rosenkavalier* at ten o'clock in the morning. This is the famous scene in which Octavian arrives to present the silver rose, sees Sophie for the first time and falls in love with her. The orchestra had had a very heavy Wagner night the previous evening and were just playing the notes, without much feeling. Kleiber let them go on for about five minutes, then stopped them, and said in his lovely broken English:

'Gentlemen. These are two little souls meeting one another for the first time. Don't shpoil it.'

"From then on we had a wonderful rehearsal.

"He had a lovely sense of humour too. One story I love and treasure: he always came round to see each artist before the performance to discuss any little details. This particular evening I was a little late getting into my costume. I was just about decent when he knocked at the door and walked straight in. I was rather taken aback and exclaimed, 'Herr Kleiber!'

" 'It's all right my dear,' he replied. 'Firstly I am short sighted, secondly I am married, and thirdly – I like it!'

"I also recall something he once said at the end of a visit to Britain. He and Ruth, his American wife, were flying to the continent from London on the same day but were going on separate planes. When I showed surprise at this, he remarked, 'I was a little orphan when I was four years old and we wouldn't want our children to be left without a parent should there be an accident.'

"No wonder we all loved him."

Constance as Octavian: her most famous role.

V

A CHAPTER OF REVIEWS

No singer – not even a Kirsten Flagstad or a Tito Gobbi – is always entirely free of faults, and every singer has his or her off days. It must also be said that opera singers tend to enrich and deepen their characterization as they grow into their roles, so that first night reviews are not always the best guide. Criticisms occasionally voiced against Constance were (1) that her vocal line was not always steady; (2) that with her operatic voice she sometimes found it hard to adapt to lieder; and (3) that in her recital work she sometimes failed to distinguish significantly between different styles and traditions. These are the inevitable risks of a large and ambitious repertoire. However even Frank Howes of *The Times* (one of her sternest critics) was prepared to acknowledge that her later recital work was good, and I have been unable to find a single serious criticism of either her Brangäne or her Octavian. There were occasional criticisms of her dramatic interpretation of certain roles but these were always in a minority. Most reviewers credited her with a very high level of dramatic talent. What is also interesting is that the American press responded quickly and warmly to her emergence as a major singer. If I have selected generously from among the most laudatory notices, this is not because

I wish to overemphasize her gifts (outstanding though these were) but because the best reviews were often the most detailed and discerning.

(Anyone wishing to skip this chapter should at least read the *Salome* reviews, if only for their entertainment value!)

TRISTAN UND ISOLDE

One can have nothing but praise ... for Constance Shacklock as Brangäne. Here is a voice that is steadily developing in power and expressiveness, one that can already be termed a dramatic contralto, and which has great potentialities. Hers was a dignified and truly satisfying performance, one that arouses the liveliest expectations for the future of this young artist – *Musical Opinion*, January 1949.

Of Constance Shacklock's Brangäne there can be nothing but praise. She easily vindicated her right to be heard and seen in the company of singers of such distinction [Flagstad and Hotter]. She sang with understanding and great sympathy, and her voice, steady and smoothly produced, was remarkably in accord with her sensitive interpretation – *Musical Opinion*, July 1949.

Constance Shacklock's Brangäne is now such an accomplished study, both vocally and dramatically, as to be worthy of a place in any company – *Musical Courier*, New York, July 1952.

IL TROVATORE

Miss Constance Shacklock now sings the part of Azucena Her voice often catches the requisite note of horror and she acts with spirit, but her youth is not to be disguised: as a witch she is not altogether convincing – *The Times*, 7 October 1948.

But it was above all to Constance Shacklock, the true star of the evening, to whom we would offer our admiration. A very attractive mezzo with the high notes well placed, she threw herself passionately into the part, giving Azucena the sorceress such a tragic quality. This was characteristic of her astonishingly eloquent performance; her voice was vibrant with harmonious poetry – *Liege Gazette* (translated), 12-13 November 1960.

On the other hand we have seldom heard an Azucena who could surpass the talent of Miss Shacklock. Her voice, her intense dramatic acting, gained everyone's approval – *La Wallone* (translated), 12-13 November 1960.

Miss Shacklock threw herself whole-heartedly into the role of Azucena. She played the part in her own way and that way was of outstanding quality. It had an unprecedented effect on the audience – *La Meuse*, Liege (translated), 14 November 1960.

DER ROSENKAVALIER

Constance Shacklock, as always, was absolutely magnificent

in the name part – *Musical Express*, 26 February 1949.

The great success of the evening was the Octavian, sung and acted by Constance Shacklock with a fine art that places her in the front rank of operatic artists. She has a lovely mezzo-soprano with a sensitive warm tone ... and is a most accomplished actress – *Musical Courier*, New York, 1 December 1949.

Shacklock as Octavian and Schwarzkopf as Sophie have already received the highest praise in this column, and this performance showed once again that even the highest praise is barely adequate. I find it impossible to imagine, for instance, 'the presentation of the rose' being better sung, while the last twenty minutes or so of the opera, which consists of a flow of inspiration in music that surely can never have been surpassed, was sung by singers who did Strauss full justice – *Musical Express*, 17 November 1950.

At Covent Garden we have seen several changes of Sophie, one of the Princess, and two of Baron Ochs over the past five or six years, but the Octavian never varies. Constance Shacklock we have come to take for granted in this role, which might have been written for her. Her every performance is a gem – *Glasgow Herald*, 15 November 1954.

Vocally, Miss Shacklock now finds the *tessitura* of the part rather high – Harold Rosenthal in *The Financial Times*, 28 May 1959.

MEISTERSINGER

We have surely never had a more charming Magdalena than Constance Shacklock – *Liverpool Daily Post*, 12 March 1949.

SALOME

Shacklock, whom we know as an admirable artist, could do nothing, poor lady, as Herodias with a headpiece like a bathing tent through which Salvador Dali expected her to sing commandingly – *The Tribune*, December 1949.

Constance Shacklock, although she takes the stage very well, had a trying time as Herodias with a miniature Punch-and-Judy show for a head-dress – *The Observer*, 13 November 1949.

Constance Shacklock appears not so much as a debauched nymphomaniac in the last stages of dissolution, as a prep school matron who has come in on unmentionable goings-on in the dorm. But then her headgear is so constructed that she is unable to move her neck, and this is not calculated to bring out the best in even the hardiest trouper – *Isis*, 23 November 1949.

Just before the opening Dali sent a demand for a "gloomy rhinoceros" to throw "a cloud of death" over Salome's dying scene. "It would be sublime," he said.

Brook – who had already ignored an idea for a flying hippopotamus – ignored this too. "The rhino was just a variation of an earlier theme," he said. This is the rhino as drawn by Dali: [then follows a sketch of what looks like a cow with a sheep's head, over which, as an evident afterthought, has been rammed a huge horn. Not one of Dali's best efforts] – *News Chronicle* 12 November 1949.

AIDA

The Covent Garden Opera presents an immensely thrilling, strident, compelling *Aida*. Saturday evening's performance at the Theatre Royal, Birmingham, was Amneris's. Constance Shacklock's singing won the most enthusiastic applause of the opera season in Birmingham – *Evening Dispatch*, Birmingham, 13 April 1953.

A special ovation was given to Constance Shacklock, who rose to great heights of poignant eloquence as Amneris – *Edinburgh Evening News*, 28 April 1950.

Constance Shacklock scored a personal triumph with her interpretation of Amneris. Possessing a flexible voice of great range and beauty, she eloquently expressed the emotions of the tormented Pharaoh's daughter. Her acting too carried complete conviction and she made the first scene of Act IV tremendously moving – *Edinburgh Evening Dispatch*, 28 April 1950.

Constance Shacklock, Amneris, was not in her best voice – Andrew Porter in *The Financial Times*, 6 January 1958.

There was much to excite in Covent Garden's new

production of *Aida* with which they opened their run at the Palace, but the eye and ear were constantly captured by Constance Shacklock, who as Amneris gave us opera at its best – voice, gesture and expression directed in a mature and unremittingly powerful appeal to the emotions. Even the tomb scene itself is a dramatic anticlimax after her poignant evocation of envy and grief when Radames is being sentenced to death. Enough to melt a sphynx – *Manchester Evening News* 18 March 1958.

BORIS GODUNOV

Constance Shacklock in the first Polish scene has the weakest music to sing in the whole opera but [she] appeared to be upset neither by this nor by the appalling backcloth – *Musical Express*, 3 November 1950.

Miss Edith Coates' Innkeeper and Miss Shacklock's Princess Marina are in their different ways accomplished musical characterizations – *The Times*, 23 October 1950.

CARMEN

The touch of distinction that it [the performance] possessed may be certainly assigned to Miss Constance Shacklock, who sang the part of Carmen for the first time [sic] – *The Times*, 24 January 1950.

Constance Shacklock, a mezzo-soprano who has made great progress and has recently achieved a notable Oktavian in *Rosenkavalier*, threw herself into the part loyally.

But as so often happens when *Carmen* is sung in English, there is a radical wrongness of timbre in the voice and what should be quick, light, and transparent becomes rich and earnest and slow. However there was much to admire. Miss Shacklock has a fine presence – *Manchester Guardian*, 14 February 1951.

The Covent garden Opera Company received a great ovation at the Empire Theatre, Edinburgh, last night for their performance of *Carmen* and much of the applause was evoked by the outstanding singing of Constance Shacklock in the name part, and Edgar Evans as Don Jose. Their dramatic finale was superbly executed – *Edinburgh Evening News*, 9 March 1951.

But now for Carmen herself. I must confess I have never yet seen a Carmen who is completely convincing, but I have, in Constance Shacklock, seen one who holds out the promise of doing full justice to this demanding role. No singer, in my opinion, could hope to be a real Carmen until she has sung it many times. It is a role that has to be 'lived'. Shacklock showed us time and time again during her performance that she is capable of attaining this. The Habañera, for instance, was sung with a lightness and seductiveness that one would not dream possible from a Wagnerian singer. I felt that if one can convince so completely in the Habañera, then the rest is bound to follow.

Shacklock's acting, and the fact that she can, and does, look a Carmen, are very great assets in her favour. It is not surprising that at present she sometimes gives the impression of being a cross between an Englishwoman and a Spanish gipsy, nor that the voice of Brangäne is sometimes heard. I would like more of the 'closed throated' sounds that she can, and does, employ so well; also there are places where the inflections could be improved. But these things are comparatively small details well within her power to accomplish, as indeed she showed us in no small degree.

To say that Shacklock is a satisfactory Carmen would be to underrate her performance, for only the most critical observer would spot the points that could be improved. Nevertheless, good as it is at the moment, I am convinced that, given sufficient opportunities of singing the role, something truly great will emerge – Malcolm Rayment in *Musical Express*, 16 March 1951.

A successful presentation [of *Carmen*] depends on the good fortune in having available a mezzo-soprano who can look the part of Carmen, act it with sultry, untamed gipsy ardour and sing it with a lively fire that smoulders always and bursts suddenly into flame. The *mezzo* voice and disposition is usually too sluggish. The present production is happy, therefore, in having a superb Carmen in Constance Shacklock. She meets all the requirements in appearance and in acting, and the burning fire in her voice, while doing full justice to the richly-charged beauty of its lower, vibrant register, never wants for the touch of the tempestuous and the brilliant spark of passion... It is a splendid performance – Frank Murphy, *Theatre* (Sydney), August 1958.

Noted English artist Constance Shacklock is the finest Carmen seen in Melbourne for many years — Linda Phillips (newspaper unidentified), August 1958.

VERDI'S REQUIEM

Especially high honours are due to Joan Hammond and Constance Shacklock. This writer cannot recall such superb Verdi singing for many years as that of Miss Hammond. Great praise also goes to Miss Shacklock — Arthur Notcutt, *Musical Courier*, New York, August 1949.

Joan Hammond I have never heard sing better, and Constance Shacklock's performance in the 'Lux Aeterna' will long live in my memory — M.R. [Malcolm Rayment], *Musical Express*, 10 June 1949.

Constance Shacklock..... was always the artist, searching with her mind into the significance behind the notes. I have seldom heard this gifted singer sound the note of heartfelt and simple unselfconscious eloquence so beautifully as this — Neville Cardus in the *Manchester Guardian*, 31 March 1956

MAGNIFICAT (VAUGHAN WILLIAMS)

The *Magnificat* ... was the most considerable work [of the evening], in which Miss Constance Shacklock was the not very satisfactory soloist. She was too often wide of the notes — up to half a tone on either side — *The Times*, 25 May 1950.

The soloist was Miss Constance Shacklock, but she had not taken its measure either in the spirit or the letter – *Musical Times*, June 1950.

[The problem may have been the modal nature of the music, which requires a different mental approach. Failing this, it is very easy to sing off-key]

GERONTIUS

Constance Shacklock, singing the Angel for the first time, left me in no doubt, following her operatic triumphs, that she is today among Britain's great singers. Except for her first 'alleluia' she invested the part's poetic cadences with a haunting loveliness – *Daily Telegraph*, 4 April 1953.

Constance Shacklock now takes her place amongst the distinguished names associated with the part of the Angel. Perhaps her voice is less "spiritual" than some we have heard in the past, but few singers have shown firmer control or have been better equipped technically for this part – *Sheffield Telegraph*, 6 April 1953.

The role of the Angel, which was so memorably sung by the late Kathleen Ferrier two years ago, was taken yesterday by mezzo-soprano Constance Shacklock. Her singing reached great heights by its striking tonal beauty. I shall long remember the way she began the section 'Softly and gently, dearly-ransomed soul' – *Evening Herald*, Dublin, 27 September 1954

This was more than just a concert: there was devotion and faith expressed in music and something quite unique. The outstanding soloists were Richard Dowd, tenor, Constance Shacklock, contralto, and Marian Nowakowski, bass. They all interpreted the work with great musical security and sensitivity. There were tremendous ovations at the end – *Berliner Morgenpost* (translated), 21 September 1956.

(Royal Festival Hall): Miss Constance Shacklock caressed the Angel's music but allowed her timbre to curdle and often pitched her line flat – *The Times*, 6 June 1957.

(Theatre Royal, Dublin): Constance Shacklock's Angel could scarcely have been sung with more understanding, bringing an almost spiritual tranquillity and tenderness to her 'farewell' – *Irish Press*, 10 June 1957.

SOLOMON

Constance Shacklock sang boldly and with a firm round tone, but both ... [the other soloists] suffered from a pervasive wobble in the voice – *Daily Telegraph*, 24 October 1955.

PROMENADE CONCERTS

Constance Shacklock sang the aria 'O Don fatale' from *Don Carlos* superbly, dominating the fairly massive orchestration with complete ease – *Musical Express*, 29 September 1950.

Miss Constance Shacklock's voice and Verdi's 'O Don

fatale' together (in the original key, *mirabile dictu*) were like some strong red wine – *The Times*, 18 September 1950.

The audience sang 'Rule Britannia' a second time, having only shortly before attempted to rival Miss Constance Shacklock's warmth of tone in that splendid arrangement of it by Sir Malcolm Sargent which so delighted the late King – *The Times*, 21 September 1951.

*

Also of course, Constance gave recitals. Here however the reviews tend to be unusually detailed and rarely lend themselves to short quotations. Her first London recital, on the stage of Covent Garden in February 1953, which was also the first of its kind at the Royal Opera House, received generally favourable notices both in Britain and the USA, although *Musical Opinion* was surely right to criticise 'her favourite stance – from which she rarely departed – of leaning on the piano at an angle roughly that of the Tower of Pisa.' (This was a favourite pose of Hollywood singers.) In 1958 she gave a notable recital in Moscow, during which a number of songs by Tchaikowsky and Rachmaninov, said to be 'most difficult pieces were rendered by her with great expressive power' (*Sovietskaya Kultura*). Two of them were sung in the original Russian. In Salisbury, Rhodesia, in November 1957, a recital by Constance provoked 'one of the greatest ovations ever given to a visiting artist' (*Salisbury Press*). Only the *Times* refused to be wooed.

Indeed it was ungracious enough to say, of her final

London recital, that 'her singing [had] needed further discipline, which she has now applied to it.' This was presumably Frank Howes, the reactionary critic who had so unnerved Karl Rankl. In those days the *Times* employed a team of musical correspondents and its reviews varied widely in tone. At least one of its critics was noted for his barbed comments, eg. 'X was below, and Y above, form.' 'Z sang well – it is his best role.' It is sad to reflect that the *Times* was often less appreciative of the best British singers than the continental presses.

As for the gramophone magazines, which did often carry reviews of live performances, their treatment of British singers was nothing short of scandalous. The blunt truth is that in those days British artists were hardly ever recorded, and full-blooded praise would have raised too many awkward questions. The problem is discussed in a later chapter.

VI

TOURS AND VISITS

In June 1952, when the Cold War was at its height, Constance hit the newspaper headlines.

It all began quietly enough. At very short notice she received a telegram from Kleiber, who was now in charge of the Berlin State Opera in the Eastern (Russian) sector of the city. He was due to conduct a performance of *Tristan und Isolde* on 15 June and his Brangäne had been taken ill. Could Constance fly out and sing the part instead? Covent Garden gave her permission to go and she went along to the Russian Embassy to see about a visa.

"I arrived at 12.15 to discover that the Embassy closed at noon. There was a cleaner washing the steps outside the building and I asked her if there was anyone on the premises as my call was urgent. She disappeared inside for quite a while and then returned to tell me that there was someone there who would see me. I was shown into a large office, in which, sitting behind a desk was a very elegant-looking portly gentleman. I told him that I had to go to Germany the next day as it was an emergency, and that I needed a visa. He was apologetic but explained that my request would have to go to Moscow. I can remember very clearly my reply:

" 'There is no time for the request to go to Moscow. I have to go tomorrow and I'm sure that Herr Kleiber would not have sent for me if it were not possible. I will go, and if I'm not allowed through the Brandenburg Gate, at least I shall have tried.'

"He gave me a very searching look, then took my hands and said, 'Good luck, my dear.' I then departed to the travel agency to get my ticket and to let Kleiber know the time of my arrival. I'd been told that he or his wife would meet me at the airport."

There was no problem with the travel documents since all flights from London to Berlin were then to Tempelhof Airport in the Western sector. Also the flight was a good one and the plane landed at Berlin ten minutes early. Constance found herself hanging about at the meeting point outside the main entrance.

The trouble began, innocently enough it seemed at the time, when a young man approached and spoke to her in perfect English. He explained that he'd heard her speaking English as she came through the check-out and wondered if he could talk to her for a few minutes as he was English himself and working in Germany.

"He asked me why I was there and what I was doing. He seemed a very charming and intelligent young man, and so I told him. He seemed very interested. Just then a large black limousine drove up, bearing Russian number plates. I had expected to see Herr Kleiber, but it was a small, rather dour-looking woman who got out of the car. She said, 'Frau Shacklock, I'm to take you to the Adlon Hotel where you will be staying.' I started to explain to her that because of the short notice I had been unable to obtain a visa for East Germany, and what was the situation? She looked at me and replied, 'I am to take you to the Adlon Hotel. Zay are my orders.' I turned to the young man, who had been listening to the conversation, and said rather jokingly, 'Well, here goes' – and got into the car.

"We sped along to the Brandenburg Gate and I wondered what would happen. The German woman produced some papers and we were allowed through.

"The next morning, in all the British newspapers, the headline read: 'English opera star kidnapped – whirled away in a black limousine bearing Russian number plates, protesting.' The charming young man had been a newspaper reporter. The telephone at home was ringing non-stop and in the end Eric began to wonder if it was really true and contacted the British Embassy, who took up the matter. Eventually he was assured that all was well."

Later that day Constance received a telegram:

> DISTURBED BY NEWS REPORT PLEASE CONFIRM THAT YOU ARE SAFE AND WELL = MOTHER

By this time she was doing her best to quell the rumour but only the (communist) *Daily Worker* and some of the provincial newspapers (including the stalwart *Nottingham Evening Post*) carried her 'indignant denials' of the kidnapping story. One national newspaper tried to extricate itself from the mess by claiming that Constance herself had been very apprehensive, and left readers to draw the conclusion that she was a political innocent. 'I have no time for politics,' she was quoted as saying. Some days later the *Evening Standard* began a short column with the question: 'What political significance is there in the appointment of Dr Erich Kleiber as musical director of the Berlin State Opera in the Russian zone of the city?' On that farcical note the story was allowed to die.

To come back to Constance's own account:

"The Adlon Hotel was just the other side of the Brandenburg Gate. It had been one of Germany's first class hotels but was now a sorry sight. The carpets were dirty and threadbare, the curtains were in poor condition and the whole atmosphere was one of neglect and sadness. Was I glad to see the Kleibers when they came to the hotel to welcome me and to arrange for the rehearsal next day at the theatre. After they had gone I returned to my room. It was a beautiful moonlit night, and looking out over what had once been the heart of the city I could see only devastation. Hardly a building was still standing. There, just ahead, was the bunker where Goebbels and his family had committed suicide when Germany was defeated. How my imagination began to run riot, and I found myself recalling some of the horrors of the war. I don't think I had much sleep that night.

"Next morning I was picked up by car and taken to the theatre to meet the other artists... I had a very short run through with the producer, Frida Leider, who had herself been a very famous Isolde. She explained the architecture of the production and that was it – there was no rehearsal. Having sung Brangäne with Kleiber so many times I did not fear the performance and in fact it was wonderful. All the artists were so helpful and kind in every way, and when it came to the final curtain calls they pushed me forward to a heart-warming ovation from the audience and a loud shout of 'Bravo Britain!' [in fact she took ten curtain calls]. The Berlin press too, were very complimentary and so I felt very proud to be the first English artist to sing in Germany after the war. When I arrived back at Heathrow[1] the following day I was greeted by about ten reporters, asking questions and taking pictures of me.

"I told them what a wonderful time I had had and of everyone's kindness, and that I would be very happy and honoured to go back there again. 'What about the kidnapping?' they demanded. I explained that this had been wrongly reported and that the German State Opera had vouched for my need to be there and that I could not have been received and treated more generously. The next day nothing of interest was reported in the papers, but a short time later a report from a foreign newspaper came to me stating that I had not been very graciously received and that I did not wish to go to Germany again. [2]

"In those days, for two guineas, you could subscribe to Durrant's Press Cuttings Agency, from which you would receive newspaper reports from anywhere in the world that bore your name. I felt quite sick at heart when I read this report – the very opposite of what I had said. I felt so strongly about it that I told my husband that I was prepared to sue them for reporting such untruths. Dear Eric, with his usual calm and foresight, remarked, 'It is your word against theirs. Are you prepared perhaps to lose the case and waste a lot of hard-earned money to justify yourself? Forgive and forget.'

"I did forgive, but to this day I am still very sceptical of press reports.

"I have many memories of that visit to East Berlin but there is one that I shall never forget. I wanted to buy some Wagner scores, which were not available at that time in England. I told Kleiber about this and he said that there was a very good music shop not far from the Opera House where he was sure I would get them. It was about six stops on the local railway and I decided to go and find it. Looking back, I realise what a great risk I was taking, having no visa and therefore no identification other than my British passport.

"When I arrived at the station in question I just couldn't believe what I was seeing. It was like a dead city. The buildings were all in ruins: street after street after street of them. I recalled the film *Things to Come* from the book by H.G.Wells. I was horrified. I was just about to return to the station to go back to the hotel when I saw a figure in the distance. Also I noticed what appeared to be some shops far ahead. I decided to go and ask the person for directions.

"She was an elderly woman and she stared at me when, in my very limited German, I asked her where the music shop was. She almost gasped, 'Englisch?' 'Ja?' I replied, and she threw her arms around me and just sobbed. It was quite a while before she would let me go. By this time, I too was crying. She pointed in the direction of the shops and then gave me a look I shall never forget. I went on my way and she watched me until I was completely out of sight. Who she was and what was in her mind when she embraced me I shall never know, but for a brief moment I felt I had met a kindred soul. That incident, and others from the same visit, are still as clear in my mind as if they happened yesterday."

*

During the first few years at Covent Garden, the company toured for six weeks of the year, visiting Leeds, Manchester, Glasgow, Edinburgh, Liverpool and Birmingham. This was an interesting experience for all of us, performing in different theatres with different acoustics and different positioning of the orchestra. Sometimes the scenery had to be adjusted considerably to fit into the smaller theatres. This all made a difference to our performance on stage and it sometimes took nearly the whole of the first act to get the 'feel' of the theatre.

"The problem with the scenery could lead to some curious effects, as when we performed *Aida* at Glasgow. In the fourth act there is a point when the slaves, naked except for scanty loin-cloths, cross the back of the stage, two tiers up, carrying heavy stones. The proscenium arch was considerably lower than at Covent Garden and all the audience saw was a lot of bent bare legs. Also I remember running onto the stage – very dramatically – and singing: 'She, my rival detested, has escaped me, and from the priesthood Radames is now awaiting the sentence of a traitor!' There were shrieks of laughter from the audience and I couldn't understand what was happening. It was very unnerving and it took me quite a few moments to compose myself. In that particular production, Amneris's costume was made of very flimsy chiffon, and under the too-powerful glare of the Glasgow stage lights all was revealed!

"During our touring time we always enjoyed our visit to Birmingham. It was a very good, spacious theatre, and the audiences were very enthusiastic. On one occasion – a *Carmen* night – my parents had travelled to Birmingham especially for the first performance. My father was not very musical but by now he was very proud of me and was happy on this occasion to accompany Mother to the opera. It was obvious that Mother had not told him the story of *Carmen*, but he seemed quite fascinated by what was happening on stage. I had just finished singing the Seguidilla and had been on stage for about half an hour, when he turned to Mother and whispered, 'When does Constance come on?'

" 'That's her on stage'.

" 'What? That hussy?'

"We had many laughs over that performance. Sitting on the other side of Mother was a very enthusiastic young opera lover who kept chatting to her. When she proudly told him that I was her daughter he insisted on sharing his box of chocolates with her, much to Mother's embarrassment and Father's questioning looks!!"

In July – August 1953 the Covent Garden Opera Company was invited to Bulawayo for the Rhodes centenary celebrations. The opera house, which had been an aircraft hangar, had been ingeniously converted into a theatre capable of holding 3000 people. Constance recalls that one-tenth of the seats, all at the back, were reserved for black people. "I felt this was so humiliating, and when I expressed – very strongly – my feelings about it, I was told that this was the first time ever that coloured people had been allowed to join a European audience in a theatre!

"Attendances averaged over 2000 a night, which was wonderful considering that this was the first time that an opera had been staged there, and that only sixty years previously Bulawayo had been a native village. Of the four operas we gave there – *Aida, Figaro, Boheme* and *Gloriana, Aida* seemed to be the favourite. I must add that our sets and costumes were magnificent and the casts were excellent.

"At first the audiences were rather apprehensive about *Gloriana* [in which Constance sang the lead role of Queen

Elizabeth I] but after the first act they realized what an exciting and dramatic opera it was, and at the end they gave us almost a standing ovation."

As part of the Festival there were many interesting exhibitions. Queueing to see one of them, Constance noticed, just in front of her, three young black men, "very smartly dressed and wearing bowler hats, which made me smile." When they reached the entrance they were told, 'Sorry, no blacks.' Constance couldn't believe her ears and questioned the attendant. 'Why?' 'Sorry,' she was told, 'that's the rule.' She replied that in that case she didn't want to see the exhibition either, and walked away. In those days it was not uncommon for Rhodesians visiting or revisiting England, to deplore South African *apartheid* and to add that, of course, there was no colour bar in Rhodesia. Constance's reminiscences tell a rather different story.

Four years later, Constance was invited back to Rhodesia to sing at a gala performance to mark the inauguration of the new Governor, Sir Peveril William Powlett. During this second visit she stayed with friends whom she had met previously at the Rhodes Festival. "They lived very near the bush country, in beautiful scenery, and they insisted I visit the woods early in the morning to see the monkeys and other wild life, as this was when they came out to feed and drink at the pools. So we duly set off at the crack of dawn with our picnic breakfast. We arrived at a lovely oasis and I started to walk around. Suddenly I saw a mother chimp sitting peacefully on a branch of a large tree, feeding her two babies." At the same moment three young men appeared out of the bush and in her excitement Constance called to them to come and see. One of them said, 'This is a long way from Nottingham, Miss Shacklock.' They were three students from her home town!

There are several foreign visits that Constance does not mention. One would love to know what she thought about Paris in June 1948, when she travelled there with the Covent Garden Company to take part in two performances of *Peter Grimes*. Several of the programmes survive among her papers. Nor does she say anything about Dublin although she appeared for three brief seasons at the Gaiety Theatre as a guest singer with the Dublin Grand Opera Society (December 1950, 1952 and 1953). On the first occasion, and at very short notice, she sang Azucena in *Il Trovatore* in place of Patricia Black, who had been called away to London. This had placed the DGOS in an awkward position and there was even talk of the performances having to be cancelled. However an appeal for help to Covent Garden was answered in the most generous terms, and both Constance and Edith Coates were immediately released to cover the vacant roles. As one Irish journal remarked, it was a fine example of standing by the old motto that the show must go on no matter where. All credit to David Webster and the Covent Garden management. In 1952 and 1953 she was invited back to sing Carmen and made a great impression. The Dublin *Evening Herald* voted her 1952 Carmen 'the best operatic performance of the year.'

(Her later overseas visits – to Buenos Aires, the USSR,

Australia and Liège in Belgium – were undertaken after she went freelance and are discussed in a later chapter. For a complete list of her UK and overseas concert engagements see Appendix B.)

---

1. Actually Northolt. Constance's memory is at fault here.

2. This, of course, is what readers expected to be told. The idea that political hostility did not extend to all aspects of life was very hard for most Westerners to grasp. In fact the USSR fostered cultural contacts as a way of improving its own image, and Russians and East Europeans knew that in that kind of context they could respond warmly and cordially without fear of censure. Additionally for Berliners of course, the visit was a psychological boost, reducing their post-war sense of isolation.

VII

ARTISTS, ACCIDENTS, ACHIEVEMENTS

Constance recalls that in the immediate post-war period all the operas were sung in English. This of course made heavy demands on foreign singers who had to learn every libretto again from scratch. "One thinks especially in this connection of *Die Meistersinger*, a very long and demanding Wagner opera where the soloists tended to be German anyway. Hans Hotter, famous for the role of Hans Sachs, Ludwig Weber, for his interpretation of Pogner, and Elizabeth Grummer – a lovely Eva – come obviously to mind. The management began to feel that if we were to become an international opera house we would have to perform the operas in the original language – which we did the very next season (1951-52). Personally I felt that this was the right decision. Translations are often quite inaccurate and this in turn affects delivery, musical phrasing and verbal emphasis."

Constance particularly admired Elizabeth Grummer. "To me, she was the perfect Eva. She looked beautiful, her clear warm soprano voice sailed through the theatre and the audiences loved her. I was singing Magdalena, and from our very first meeting there was a rapport between us which clearly showed in our performances together. One day, during a coffee break, she showed me a photograph of herself with her husband and their two small children –

such a happy group. I remember saying how much they must miss her when she was away singing and I asked whether her husband was musical. Her reply shook me. 'He was killed during the war.' My heart went out to her. It must have taken great courage to come and sing in the country that had deprived her of a loving partner. But she was a great person and this came over very strongly in her performances."

In the summer of 1951 a new production of *Meistersinger* was launched under the baton of Sir Thomas Beecham. Beecham had been excluded from Covent Garden for many years and although he could still produce the old magic his powers of concentration were not quite what they had been. The result was an opening night destined to be long remembered, though not for the usual reasons. Constance in particular had good cause to feel unnerved. "In the second act, Pogner, Eva's father, sings a very beautiful aria just before he enters the house. Pogner was being played by Ludwig Weber and Beecham had a great admiration for Weber's artistry. Predictably he sang the aria magnificently, and Beecham stood there, smiling at the orchestra in approval, forgetting that Eva and Magdalena come round from the back of the house at this point and have a recitative dialogue for about ten bars before the orchestra comes in and the scene continues. Alas, no orchestra did come in. Elizabeth Grummer and I started to improvise, trying frantically to keep things going, and just hoping that at some point the orchestra would come to our rescue. Unfortunately when he came out of his reverie, Beecham, bemused by the unfamiliar dialogue and assuming that we'd lost our place in the score, turned to the Leader of the orchestra, Charles Taylor, and in a loud voice exclaimed, ' Good God, Taylor, where the hell are they?' Next day, one of the newspapers reported that two operas had been performed at Covent Garden the previous evening: one on the stage and one in the pit, and that it was a pity they didn't get together more often. I can smile now, when I recall it all, but it was quite frightening at the time, and it must have looked and sounded very odd."

Of all her operatic roles, Constance felt that Carmen was the most challenging. "Merimée, in his novel, depicts her as a real slut but Bizet did not write sluttish music, and for a long time I could not tie up the music with Carmen's character. I think that eventually I must have done so because I held the record for the number of performances in the role at Covent Garden."

Carmen also gave her some nerve-racking moments. On one occasion Edgar Evans, who was due to sing Don José, was taken ill very suddenly and Jon Vickers stepped in at the eleventh hour. "If I remember rightly he was over here from his home in Canada to sing Peter Grimes.

"He had never seen the sets and we had no chance to rehearse. He was simply shown the exits. The performance was electrifying. We had to watch each other like cat and mouse and our reactions were absolutely spontaneous. In the last scene of the opera, when Carmen rejects José – having switched her affections to the Torreador – José stabs her. This was so real that it produced a deathly

Constance as Carmen: Kirov Theatre Leningrad, 8th February 1957

stillness in the theatre – I'm sure that for a moment they all thought he had actually killed me. Then, tremendous applause: an unforgettable performance!"

Unforgettable for a different reason was another performance, this time with Jimmy Johnston in the role of Don José. "In the third act, when emotions between Carmen and José are running high, Carmen pulls out her dagger. At that moment Jimmy stood up unexpectedly and my dagger caught his eye. Blood began to pour down his face. I was horrified. Had I blinded him? From the looks on the faces of the chorus and the hushed silence in the auditorium most people seemed to think I had. Fortunately it was at the end of the act and almost immediately the curtain came down. The dagger had caught him just below the eyebrow where the skin is very thin – just missing the eyeball. For the rest of the evening there was a greatly relieved Carmen, but I didn't sleep much that night. Thereafter I took great care when drawing my dagger."

In 1955 Constance celebrated her 500th performance at Covent Garden, having never missed a performance in nine seasons. "It became quite a joke among the artists in the company. If they were asked who they were understudying and replied 'Shacklock,' they were told, 'You're all right. You'll never have to go on. She's never ill.' Like an athlete, over the years one builds up a great mental and physical strength with the added joy of loving one's work.[1]

"It was during that season that my mental strength was

very much tested. It was the Last Night of the Proms. I was to sing 'Rule Britannia!' and Gina Bachauer the Greek pianist was to play the Grieg Piano Concerto. At the rehearsal in the morning she was greatly distressed as she had received an anonymous note saying that if she played that evening she would be shot. She was greatly perturbed and said she could not perform. I found myself assuring her that if anyone really intended to shoot her they wouldn't tell her; they would just do it. It was just some sadistic attempt to ruin her performance. After reassurance from everyone, and knowing that we were all supporting her, like the great artist that she was, she agreed to perform. The police were called in and took up strategic positions in every corner of the Albert Hall. It was a very tense moment when she went on to the platform.

"After a very heart-warming reception, she poised herself at the piano and started to play. The performance was going beautifully when, in one of the soft, velvety passages of the second movement, someone burst a balloon. For a moment she almost jumped out of her skin and then, with great courage and dignity, continued to play. What an ovation she received and how I admired her pluck."

Constance's association with the Last Night of the Proms was of course very special. Under the baton of Sir Malcolm Sargent she sang 'Rule Britannia!' on no less than ten occasions – a record that has never been equalled. To be invited to perform at the Last Night is a great honour anyway, and to do so year after year speaks volumes for Constance's reputation and popularity with the promenaders. 'She *was* Britannia' is a comment still sometimes heard. "To know that one's voice was heard by 5000 people in the Albert Hall and that it was relayed by radio to six continents was one of the highlights of my career," she later confessed. "How privileged I was. Sir Malcolm was wonderful to work with. The promenaders loved him and so did I. A story was once told to me which I can't authenticate but which, knowing his generous nature, I believe to be true. I understand that he lost a teenage daughter with polio. During one of the prom seasons a young boy, also a polio victim, wrote to Sir Malcolm and told him how much joy the music gave him. A friendship ensued, and when eventually the boy also died, his parents asked if they could supply the carnations which Sir Malcolm always wore when conducting at the Proms – a gesture which, I'm told, touched him deeply." [2]

A conductor's *rapport* with a singer is immensely important, both in terms of performance and also for the effect it can have on a singer's career. Conductors can and often do suggest particular artists, and their requests are usually heeded. Sir Malcolm Sargent, Sir John Barbirolli, Karl Rankl, and of course Erich Kleiber all admired Constance's singing, and the number of engagements which she had with these conductors tells its own tale. After being more or less pushed out of Covent Garden, Rankl became the principal conductor of the Scottish National Orchestra, and thereafter Constance became a familiar figure on the platform of the Usher Hall Edinburgh, St Andrew's Hall Glasgow, and various Scottish town halls.

Rankl's admiration for Constance bore fruit in another way. Rankl may not have been the ideal conductor for Covent Garden but he was entirely at home with *avant garde* music and as a young man he had been Schoenberg's favourite pupil. In recognition of this, the BBC invited him to conduct two performances of Schoenberg's elaborate and difficult *Gurrelieder* [3] with the BBC Chorus and the Royal Philharmonic Orchestra (the first time, incidentally, that the work had been broadcast in the UK). Constance was offered the part of the wood dove. "It was," she recalls, "one of the biggest challenges of my career."

At first she declined. "When they told me that it was by Schoenberg my reply was, 'No thank you. I have no feeling whatsoever for that kind of music. It's agony to learn, agony to sing, and gives me no satisfaction at all.' I was assured that it was very like Wagner, especially *Tristan and Isolde*, and would I at least look at it before saying no? They (the BBC) were quite sure I would change my mind. Well, Eric and I did go over the score quite a few times and although it looked formidable I finally decided I would learn it. I must admit that in the end, and to my very great surprise, I loved it. The other soloists were Sylvia Fisher, Raymond Nilsson, Dennis Stephenson and Owen Brannigan, and the speaker was the well-known BBC announcer, Alvar Liddell. Two and a half years later we performed it at the Edinburgh Festival and it received a great ovation. It was performed at the Proms last season (1997) and it was a great thrill to be there and to hear it again. I kept asking myself how did I ever learn such a difficult score and sing it from memory? Eric must have spent many patient hours teaching it to me."

At this distance of time it is worth recalling some of the review comments since they help to dispel traditional prejudices. *The Listener* thought that Dr Rankl was 'to be congratulated on a really splendid performance, to which everybody contributed – notably Miss Fisher and Miss Shacklock....' Similarly Martin Cooper in *The Spectator*: 'Beauty and intensity of tone are all important for this music, and under Karl Rankl the Royal Philharmonic Orchestra played with a power and a finish worthy of Schoenberg's richly laden style. Sylvia Fisher and Constance Shacklock were wholly at their ease....' Two years later, when the work was repeated at the Edinburgh Festival, it was Constance who, in review after review, was acclaimed the star of the evening. 'Of the soloists, Constance Shacklock was outstanding' (*Daily Worker*, 26 August 1954). 'It was not until Constance Shacklock, the wood dove, announced love's death that the score came vocally fully alive' (*Bulletin and Scots Pictorial*). 'Constance Shacklock was powerful and darkly impressive' (*Scottish Daily Mail*). 'Much the best solo singing came from Miss Shacklock' (*Birmingham Post*, 27 August). Finally the Edinburgh *Evening News* noted that ' of the entire company, Constance Shacklock alone sang without a copy.'

A composer who provided difficulties of a different order was Alban Berg, though Constance seems never to have taken part in a performance of any of his major works. However Kleiber, when he was at Covent Garden, conducted ten performances of *Wozzeck*, and Constance confessed to him that she found it excruciating to listen to. His reply was that Wozzeck is going through excruciating mental experiences and that the music is designed to express it. 'You cannot write beautiful music to express this man's mental torture. Listen carefully and try to understand what the music is saying about the experience.' Constance did so, actually attending all ten performances and found, in the end, that she was living the music and that indeed it made excellent sense.

To the majority of music lovers, Constance was not first and foremost an opera singer (though opera was always her first love) but a concert artist with an especial gift for oratorio. This doubtless reflects the fact that she was seen and heard on the concert platform by a much wider section of the musical public than ever found its way to Covent Garden. In particular she became the almost automatic alto choice in major performances of Elgar's *Dream of Gerontius* and the Verdi *Requiem*, which also happened to be her favourite choral works. Her tremendous success as the Angel in *Gerontius* (which she sang for the first time in 1953)[4] was at least partly owing to her instinctive understanding of the way in which Elgar linked words and music, weaving his melodies out of the natural rise and fall of the voice when the text is read aloud. This particularly suited Constance's dramatic talent and gave to her interpretation of the part an ineffably tender quality, which was further enriched by her rare warmth of tone.

Of her second love, the Verdi *Requiem*, she recalls especially the June 1949 performance at the Royal Albert Hall under

Victor de Sabata. "When it came to the *Dies Irae* I have never heard such sounds coming from the big bass drum. It was quite terrifying. I think the audience felt it too because there was a silence in the Albert Hall which one very rarely feels. In fact the whole performance was electrifying. Martin Cooper, writing next day in the *Daily Herald* thought it the greatest performance since Toscanini's in 1938.

"At first I felt that de Sabata did not like my voice because I could not give him the heavy chest sounds required for the lower dramatic notes which the Italian singers use. This is part of their technique. But my fears were dispelled when I started to sing *Lux Eterna,* which is one of the most difficult passages for the Mezzo to control, as it starts on D above middle C, marked *ppp,* and rises to F sharp, still *ppp*. On that occasion however it just seemed to flow out and I was surprised and thrilled myself. De Sabata gently put his fingers to his lips, kissed them, and blew into space – a gesture which touched me greatly. Then, when I was joined by the tenor and bass, we seemed to achieve the perfect balance. I can still hear that trio in my mind after all these years."

Constance was a natural raconteur and one can only regret that her embryonic autobiography is so incomplete. Some of her more bizarre experiences at Covent Garden we know about only from other sources – like the time when she and Edgar Evans were obliged to rehearse a scene from *Boris Godunov* in front of the safety curtain. Cramped for space, and concentrating on his acting, Edgar Evans took one step too many and fell headlong into the open prompt box! – fortunately escaping with nothing more serious than a badly bruised knee.[5] Another unfortunate incident, reported by the *Evening Standard* (20 June 1950), occurred during a performance of *Das Rheingold* when Blanche Turner, in the role of the goddess Freya, slipped as she ran across the stage and suffered a complete blackout. 'Dramatically the collapse fitted the story: for Freya is terrified at the prospect of being carried off by the giants Fafner and Fasolt. So the audience suspected nothing wrong.

'Wotan and Fricka (Miss Constance Shacklock) picked Miss Turner up and sat her on the stage rocks. One of the Rhinemaidens crawled behind the rocks, bringing Miss Turner brandy in a drinking horn used as a stage prop.'

Catastrophe was narrowly averted, as Miss Turner later explained. 'As I was coming round, I thought of my mother, listening on the radio. I knew if I missed my next cue she would be terribly worried. I just managed to sing the phrase as it came.'

---

1. By this time Constance was a Christian Scientist and never visited a doctor. Lord Harewood called her remarkable record a case of 'mind over matter' (see *Edgar Evans Extempore* by Robert Little, St Albans 2005, p.81).

2. Sargent's daughter Pamela did die of polio in 1944. *The Dictionary of National Biography* comments that for months he was almost a broken man and that there were works which he never conducted

again except as a kind of memorial to Pamela. He made many generous but strictly private benefactions to polio victims and the carnation story is entirely in character.

3. 'The name is derived from Gurre, an ancient castle to the north of Copenhagen. The music combines the chromatic harmonies of Wagner with the polyphonic complexity of Brahms; yet the thought is no pastiche of either, and the whole work is an astonishing production, especially for a young man of twenty-six' – Humphrey Searle in the *Radio Times*, 4 January 1952.

4. Replacing Kathleen Ferrier, who was too ill to perform and who died later that year.

5. *Edgar Evans Extempore*, p.110.

VIII

FREELANCE

At the end of the 1955-56 season, Constance resigned from the Covent Garden company and went freelance. This did not put an end to her association with the Royal Opera House for she continued to be engaged by the management, though with decreasing frequency, for the next four years, after which she ceased to be available. But the reasons for her resignation remain obscure. Whether she felt that the time was now ripe to launch out on her own or whether Covent Garden was becoming a less desirable workplace is not easy to say. There is no suggestion of any crisis or indeed any reference to the matter in her autobiographical jottings. Norman Lebrecht hints at differences with Covent Garden's recently appointed musical director, Rafael Kubelik:

> There was also disaffection within. Shacklock, a company founder, resigned at the end of Kubelik's first season to pursue a freelance life that took her to the Bolshoi and the West End …. 'I didn't find Kubelik warm,' she said. 'I can't say that I didn't get on with him but we weren't on the same wavelength…' [1]

Yet Constance does not say that she resigned because of Kubelik and frankly it seems unlikely. Going freelance in the opera world at that time, and for a British singer of even Constance's ability, was an immensely risky business. It is hard to believe that she would have done so without some encouragement and promise of support. But from whom?

The only evidence we possess is purely circumstantial. Sixteen months before Constance left Covent Garden, Erich Kleiber resigned as conductor of the Berlin State Opera in protest against political interference. In August 1966 – ie. one month after the expiry of Constance's contract – he was due to conduct five performances of *Der Rosenkavalier* at Teatro Colón, Buenos Aires (where he had been a regular guest conductor during the Hitler years) and Constance was engaged to sing the role of Octavian. What other projects he had in mind and how much they involved Constance we shall never know because on 27 January 1956 Kleiber died of a heart attack while taking a bath in a hotel in Zurich. At the very least, Constance lost a good friend, an inspiring mentor, and her staunchest professional advocate.

And advocacy was what she most needed. When Constance sang in Buenos Aires they asked her, 'Are there any more like you in England?' and she replied 'Lots!' In 1962, Herbert von Karajan, conducting at the Salzburg Festival, asked Geraint Evans the same question.[2] The sad truth is that in those days, British singers were unknown internationally because their voices were hardly ever recorded. This was chiefly the fault of Walter Legge, manager of the HMV Columbia label and founder of the Philharmonia Orchestra. A man of great musical ability in other respects, Legge was stubbornly prejudiced against British artists and engaged foreign singers for all his opera recordings. According to Constance, Kleiber once said to him: 'Your recording companies are crazy. In England at the moment you have the finest trio in the world. I should know because I conduct it.' He was referring to the *Rosenkavalier* trio: Sylvia Fisher (the Marschallin), Constance (Octavian), and the Danish soprano Ruth Guldbaek (Sophie). He added: 'Strauss wanted a violin, viola and cello quality, and those three voices are the perfect blend.' [3] But his remarks fell on deaf ears.

Recordings were not the only problem. Constance was an operatic mezzo, and the mezzo voice is perforce less brilliant than the soprano. Hence there are relatively few major mezzo roles in the operatic canon. As for other conductors, Rankl did in fact help her when he moved from Scotland to Australia but Barbirolli and Sargent were first and foremost orchestral conductors who rarely ventured into opera, and during this period neither of them conducted opera abroad.

To start with, and despite Kleiber's death, things went well and luck seemed to be on her side. Speaking of the Buenos Aires *Rosenkavalier* she remarks: "I was thrilled to learn that my other colleagues were to be the Swedish soprano Birgit Nilsson as the Marschallin, Emmy Looser from the Vienna State Opera as Sophie, and Lorenzo Alvery from the

Metropolitan Opera New York as Baron Ochs. I felt so honoured to be involved and that it amounted to a recognition of British opera singers. I was given to understand that I was the first British artist to sing there for over thirty years. How excited I was – until dear Kleiber passed on with a heart attack. Would the performance be cancelled? Then I heard that Ferdinand Leitner from Stuttgart was to conduct ….. In fact the first performance was cancelled at the request of the orchestra. My husband told me afterwards that on the first night-that-should-have-been he had very little sleep thinking about me, but slept soundly the following night – our actual first night! We had a good laugh over this."

Rosenkavalier was performed four times (28 August; 5, 7 and 8 September) and without exception the reviews sang Constance's praises. The *Buenos Aires Musical* went so far as to say that 'since the unforgettable times of Risë Stevens we have not seen in the Colón such a true Octavian.' This was also the first time that she had sung the part in the original German. Then, with scarcely a break, it was back to England and the Albert Hall for her now traditional appearance at the Last Night of the Proms (she had already sung the Verdi *Requiem* there with Joan Hammond on 20 July). Three days later she was in Berlin for two performances of *Gerontius*, conducted by Herbert Bardgett in the absence of Barbirolli, who was convalescing after an illness (great praise for all the soloists). Then followed an unexpected engagement at the Wexford Festival, where Flotow's *Martha* was being staged.

"Monica Sinclair, one of my colleagues at Covent Garden, had been engaged to sing the part of Nancy but was unfortunately taken ill only a few days before the first performance. I was asked to step in, which was quite a challenge as I had never sung the role before. Thanks to Eric, who worked non-stop with me for two days, I managed to learn it – something I could never have done without his help.

"When I arrived in Wexford I had no idea where the Theatre Royal was and took a taxi which went down a very narrow street and had to drive on the pavement if it met any on-coming traffic. We were held up several times. I remarked to the taxi driver that you'd think they'd make it a one-way street. He replied:

'Lady, this is the only street unless you drive on the seafront.'

"The Theatre Royal held an audience of 385 and the stage was barely 20 feet square – a little strange after working at Covent Garden – but Peter Potter, the producer, worked miracles with the crowd scenes. The other artists were so kind and helpful and were lovely to work with." She adds that the Festival was doing great work, bringing opera to this rather remote area – "and how much it was appreciated." Among Constance's papers is a visiting card inscribed: 'To Constance Shacklock, with the admiration and warmest best wishes of Compton Mackenzie – Wexford 1956.' Mackenzie, then at the height of his fame thanks to the film version of his novel *Whisky Galore*, was the Festival President.

*

From the Theatre Royal Wexford to the Kirov Theatre Leningrad and the Bolshoi Theatre Moscow may sound rather improbable but for the moment at least, Constance's star was in the ascendant. We thus come to what many would regard as the summit of her career: a joint tour of the Soviet Union with husband Eric and the soprano Joan Hammond. There were recitals and concerts (with Eric as accompanist) but the highlights of the tour for both singers were their four stage appearances. Constance sang Amneris in *Aida* at the Bolshoi Theatre Moscow, the Kirov Theatre Leningrad, and the Opera House in Riga, and the title role in *Carmen* at the Kirov. Joan Hammond sang Tatiana in *Eugen Onegin* (in Russian) at the Mali Theatre Leningrad, and the title role in all three performances of *Aida*. They were the first British artists to visit the Soviet Union after the war. How did it happen? Constance explains:

"Eric and I had given a Sunday recital at Covent Garden. We were the first to hold these concerts, which are now quite frequent and very popular. Shortly afterwards we received a letter from Alan Bush, President of the Society for Cultural Relations between Russia and England, asking if we would give a recital to their club. As it was for closer relations with the Russian people we said we would be happy to do so. I must admit, at the time it seemed a very odd little affair. There were about thirty people there in the small hall in Kensington and we wondered how they would react to a ninety minute recital. We decided we would give them the same programme as at Covent Garden, and rather to our surprise it was very warmly received. When Alan Bush thanked us, he said, 'You should go to Russia, Miss Shacklock. They would love you.'

"On the way home I said to Eric rather naughtily, 'Well, that's the last we shall hear of that!' Nine months later we were in Moscow. It made me realise that whether one is performing to five people or five thousand one must always be a perfectionist. One never knows who is listening or what may be the outcome."

Travel, they say, broadens the mind, and this was certainly true of the Aeroflot flight from Helsinki to Moscow. Joan Hammond later recalled fumbling for her safety belt whereupon 'the air hostess hastened to assure me that they were not needed – and indeed, there were none provided!

'It was strange at first also, to see passengers moving about during take off and landing. However one soon forgot our western drill, and with a feeling of being rather a devil, I decided to move about myself to see if it made any appreciable difference to the smoothness. Nothing untoward occurred, and the novelty soon wore off!' [4]

Two days later, on February 6, Constance gave her first recital of the tour in Leningrad's Kapella Hall, singing operatic arias and Russian and German songs in their original languages.

"At first the applause was respectful but, it seemed, a little reserved. But after my second group, in which I sang Rachmaninov's 'Spring Waters' and 'In the Silent Night' in Russian, all barriers were swept away, and from then onwards there was no lack of warmth. Again and again the clapping settled down into that slow, rhythmic beat which, from Russians, means absolute approval.

"Half-way through the concert both Eric and I were given large baskets of flowering plants which then stayed on the platform for the rest of the concert.

"The whole of this first experience of a Russian audience was a wonderful and exciting time, and at the end a large part of the audience crowded in a solid block in front of the platform, applauding and shouting phrases in English such as 'We have taken you to our hearts!' and 'Thank you for coming!' – a demonstration that we found infinitely moving.

"Then came my first appearance in opera in Russia, in *Carmen*, at the lovely Kirov Theatre – known in former days as the Maryinsky – on February 8. There was no time for a full rehearsal; I had only one piano-cum-production run through, and before I came on stage just before each act, I had not even seen the settings. I was fortunate in having as my Don José an excellent tenor and fine artist, Gavrilkin, who spoke English fluently. Each of us seemed to sense what the other was about to do, and that took away any slight sense of nervousness that was natural in strange surroundings.

"The production was novel to me in many ways. A striking difference from what I had been accustomed to was the playing out of the final quarrel scene between Carmen and Don José in the last Act, in front of a drop-cloth representing the entrance to the bullring. Immediately Carmen was stabbed this was 'flown' to reveal the whole arena crowded with spectators, in full sight of whom Carmen staggers in and dies at the feet of the triumphant Escamillo.

"Two days later, on Saturday February 10, *Aida* was given in the same theatre – in Russia, theatres are open on Sundays, most of them giving matinees also on that day, and are usually closed on Mondays.

"In this production Joan Hammond and I sang in Italian, the rest of the cast singing in Russian. And as well as on the stage there was international collaboration in the prompter's box, which on this occasion had to accommodate two people: the Russian prompter for the local cast, and Eric, who prompted in Italian for Joan and myself.

"Again there was a magnificent ovation which seemed as though it would never end; and we were only allowed to leave the stage finally after we had recited, in Russian, the words we had learnt for 'Thank you very much' and 'Goodnight.'

"On February 13 we flew to Riga on the Baltic. One performance of *Aida* was planned but it was completely sold out, and so many people were turned away from the box-office that we were asked to make an extra appearance in a joint recital in the same theatre.

"We began at three in the afternoon, and at 5.30 we were still going strong, and feared that the stage staff under its woman stage manager would never be able to get the stage set for the elaborate production of *Ivan Susanin* that was being given that night at 7.30 in honour of the centenary of the death of Mikhael Glinka. We were told that we had been the first British singers to appear in Riga since Joseph Hislop sang there some thirty years previously. And we were both touched to find, on leaving the theatre, a great crowd of people who had waited in pouring rain and sleet to cheer us.

"On February 17 we flew south to Moscow, and two days later I gave my first recital in the large and beautiful Tchaikowsky Hall, specially designed for recitals. Many singers and musicians from the Bolshoi Theatre came to the concert, among them Russia's famous tenor Ivan Kovlovsky, who came afterwards to my dressing-room and congratulated me. Incidentally part of the concert was filmed.

"But of all our exciting experiences the highlight was the gala performance of *Aida* at the Bolshoi Theatre, in which both Joan Hammond and I appeared – the first time that British artists had ever sung there. For this performance we had a piano rehearsal and a dress rehearsal with full cast and orchestra. But at neither rehearsal was there any scenery – just a few props to show the outline of things. The sets – which I can only describe as MASSIVE – were only put in place for the performance itself. The fourth Act, which is the big dramatic scene for Amneris and the Priest, had three tiers, the top tier almost touching the ceiling of the theatre. (When I add that the Bolshoi proscenium has a width of 75 feet as compared to Covent Garden's 43 feet, and that the height is in proportion, you will have some idea of the scale.) I had no idea from which side or on which tier the priests would be entering or leaving and I began to feel a little anxious. The great Russian bass Ivanov, singing the role of Ramphis the high priest, could see the perplexity on my face and guided me through the whole Act with his eyes. He was just wonderful; I should have been completely lost without him.

"The *Moscow News* reported next day that there had been fifteen curtain calls, and as soon as this excitement was over we had to face a prolonged ovation back-stage from hundreds who had taken part – chorus and ballet and stage-hands. The whole experience was something I shall never forget." [5]

*

After returning to the UK, Constance plunged back into a fairly heavy concert programme. 1957 was the centenary of the birth of the composer, Edward Elgar, and in addition to the usual round of engagements there were several performances of *Gerontius*, including a notable one in Rome

– the first time that the work had ever been performed in Italy. Jon Vickers sang Gerontius, Marian Nowakowski the Priest and the Angel of the Agony, and Constance, as usual, sang the part of the Angel. Sir John Barbirolli conducted the Rome Orchestra and an Italian choir. "The diction of the choir was impeccable, and when William Walton (the composer) heard the live relay he enquired which English choir was singing it. Praise indeed! That particular performance has now been released on CD." [6]

The other significant event of 1957 was the one-week concert tour of Rhodesia mentioned in Chapter 6, which commenced with a gala performance in Bulawayo to mark the inauguration of a new Governor-General. In strictly operatic terms the year had not been very productive, despite the Russian tour, but it ended with a series of engagements at Covent Garden which extended well into 1958. By this time too there was a lengthy tour of Australia in prospect. Nevertheless the lack of opera engagements had evidently begun to worry Constance, for in July 1957 she had written to Ferdinand Leitner of Stuttgart, the conductor whom she had worked with at Teatro Colón, to ask if there were likely to be any openings for her in West Germany. Leitner regretted that in Stuttgart 'all our plans are already made' but he promised to speak to 'two or three of the principal opera agents here.' Actually it was a bad time to write since, by the time he was able to reply, her diary was already heavily booked for 1958. But there were no offers from Stuttgart in the longer term.

For the moment however these clouds were still on the

horizon, and in fact 1958 was to prove the most successful year of her freelance career. There were the usual Easter oratorios under Barbirolli (*Gerontius* in Sheffield; *Messiah* in Manchester) and then in May she travelled to the USA to sing at the Bethlehem Bach Festival ("I thought at first I was going to the Holy Land," she later confessed, "and was surprised to find there was a Bethlehem in the USA"). Bethlehem Pennsylvania is not a particularly large town but it has always been an important musical centre and its internationally famous Bach Festival was then in its fifty-first year. During her stay, Constance sang the *B Minor Mass* three times (once in St Louis and twice at Bethlehem) and the *St John Passion* twice. Normally the orchestra would have been the celebrated Philadelphia but it was just then touring Europe and so a special Festival Orchestra was assembled for the occasion. *Musical America* thought 'their far sturdier and more forthright playing much better suited to Bach than the highly perfumed and polished work of the virtuosic Philadelphia musicians.' Hugh Ross, conductor of the Schola Cantorum of New York thought the performances of the B Minor Mass 'magnificent – the finest I've heard, and I've been coming to Bethlehem for years.'

Constance admits that she did not find Bach easy to sing. "My husband used to play Bach so beautifully and with such expression on the organ. Why couldn't I express it in the same way vocally? After much pondering I realized that Bach expresses himself exclusively through the music: the text is a mere peg. Being a lover of poetry and words I did not find him satisfying until I could accept this and treat my voice as a mere instrument. This was an excellent discipline for my technique, but I must confess I preferred works in which the words were as important as the music. I'm sure this is why I loved opera so much."

*

From the USA, Constance flew directly to Australia "where I had been invited to perform for six months with the newly-formed Elizabethan Opera Company to sing Carmen, and Ortrud in *Lohengrin*." The new musical director was Karl Rankl, fresh from Scotland, and it was doubtless to Rankl that she owed her engagement. Despite his rather pernickety manner he had a real admiration for Constance's talents and proved a good friend to her over the years. "Also invited was Raymond Nilsson, who was going to sing Don José. Ray and I had sung *Carmen* many times together at Covent Garden, so there would be no need for extensive rehearsals – only for those necessary to familiarize us with the production differences. Also we had both worked extensively with Rankl, and knew what to expect musically. The opening night of the season was in Brisbane and the opera was *Carmen*. The Australian soprano who was to sing Micaela was Joy Mammen, making her debut. I felt there was great promise in this young singer. She had not only a very good voice but also an excellent stage presence. She is now a very well known teacher of singing and a Professor at the Royal Academy of Music in London.

"The opera was a great triumph but what I remember

most clearly was the terrific heat. It was even hotter than Rhodesia when I was there, and at the end of the performance I was completely exhausted. I am happier in a more temperate climate, especially when singing. There was another problem too. In all my roles (except *Boris Godunov*, when I was able to use my own hair) I had to be a brunette, and so my wigs were a very important part of my wardrobe and I had taken them with me from Covent Garden. In fact they were very valuable. Suddenly my Carmen wig disappeared. The police were called in since it was thought that it had been 'souvenired' and there was not time to get a replacement from London. A blonde Carmen was out of the question. Fortunately it was discovered. It had been collected by mistake by a dresser and taken, along with other wigs, to the chorus wardrobe. I must admit that for a short while there were panic stations.

"The next opera was *Lohengrin*. Apart from myself the cast was entirely Australian: Elizabeth West as Elsa, Neil Easton as Telramund, and Ronald Dowd as Lohengrin. The part of Ortrud was a great challenge vocally as it has a very extensive range and her character is, as one of the newspapers put it, the 'incarnation of evil' – a great acting role which, I must confess, I much enjoyed playing. Later, an Australian lady visited me at Covent Garden and said she would never forget my performance in the first Act of *Lohengrin*. I was greatly surprised as I do not sing one note in the first Act: it is all ensemble. I am on stage listening and reacting to a crowd of Counts and Nobles all arguing about who is the rightful heir to the Duchy of Brabant. Not wishing to be impolite I asked how she could remember me when I didn't sing. She replied, 'I know. It was your facial expressions and bodily reactions. They were terrifying!'

"One of my treasured memories of Brisbane was visiting the Koala Sanctuary with Ronald Dowd. We were met at the entrance by the Head Keeper and a beautiful Alsatian dog with a koala on its back, and the Keeper, still accompanied by the Alsatian, showed us around. In one big cage were about thirty koalas – expectant mothers we were told. As we walked, we chatted, and the Keeper asked why we were in Brisbane. Ronald explained that we were with the opera company. The Keeper replied, 'Wonderful. I saw *Carmen* last night and I was so thrilled.' Ronald pointed to me and said, 'There's your Carmen.' His face expressed absolute disbelief, and it took some time to convince him that the blonde lady he was now looking at had been the sultry brunette of the previous night. When he'd got over the shock, he said, 'We had a baby koala born here this morning. Please may I call her Connie, after you?' Now I have always liked my Christian name, Constance, but could never bear being called Connie. However the Keeper said that Constance was such a mouthful for that wee thing and could I be persuaded to make an exception? So somewhere in the Australian bush there is a dear koala – called Connie!

"The opera company spent four weeks in Brisbane, four weeks in Adelaide, five in Melbourne and six weeks in Sydney. Of the four cities, Sydney, for me, was the highlight in every way. We had marvellous audiences, a good theatre, and I loved the city with its wonderful

A koala called Rex (photo: Capitol Studios, Brisbane)

harbour. Only a few miles away are the famous Genolian Caves and the Blue Mountains. I could happily have settled in Sydney had Eric felt that he could join me. But he was so involved with Covent Garden that he felt that London was his rightful place. It was at that time that plans were being considered for the new opera house in Sydney. When I see pictures of it now, I think of those early pioneering days. It's good that Australia now has its own international opera house which attracts famous singers from all over the world and I feel very proud to be one of its founder members.

"On the way home from Australia I stayed briefly in Singapore, with friends who were responsible for most of the musical events there. They had a lovely home with everything in it for their comfort (running water, air conditioning), but it saddened me greatly to look out of the window and see down the street the poorer people bringing buckets and pitchers to collect water from a communal water tap at the side of the road. There was a lot of poverty there at that time, but I understand from students coming over to study at Kingston University that things are very different now and that cultural standards are very high. The recital I gave there was well attended, and a great success according to the critics. As a treat, my friends took me to a Chinese opera. It was beautifully staged and costumed but the singing made my throat ache! – a very different technique from ours though very interesting.

"By this time I was longing to get home, having been away for nearly seven months. I have always loved my home but never did it seem more precious than when I had been away for so long. I missed my husband very much but I knew that he was being looked after wonderfully by his mother, who was then living with us and had her own apartment in our home, so I had no worries on that score.

"In January 1959 *Salome* was again revived at Covent Garden, with Helga Pilarczyk, the German soprano as Salome, Otakar Kraus as Jokanaan, Erich Witte as Herod, and myself as Herodias. Pilarczyk was a great success as Salome, the avid child whom Strauss imagined slim, capricious, wanton. We were still doing this opera in English and I admired so much the foreign artists who had to learn it from scratch, and who performed it with such conviction. I still remember vividly the first two lines I sang to Herod: 'You must not look at her. Always at her do you look.'

"Like Ortrud, Herodias was a very challenging part to portray – she is such an evil woman, and the sadistic expression on her face when the head of John the Baptist is brought up and presented to Herod should make the audience loathe her (which they did!) I knew I had a vivid imagination but I never realized I was capable of portraying evil with such conviction – and enjoyment!

"The sets [and costumes] had been modified quite a bit from Dali's original conception but they were still very stark and unreal. However Strauss wonderfully expresses the feelings and emotions of each character. At first I did not find the music easy to learn but if one studies it with the libretto always in mind things fall gradually into place, including some of the unusual harmonies. Once learnt, it stays with you always."

Apart from Salome there were five performances of *Aida* with Constance in the usual role of Amneris, and three performances of *Rosenkavalier*. Also, in the autumn of 1960, she sang Azucena in two performances of *Il Trovatore* at the Theatre Royal, Liège, in Belgium. But the engagements were drying up, as the following table shows. New artists were beginning to make their mark, and at 47, Constance was getting a little old for youthful roles like Octavian and Amneris. Already, in 1959, Joan Sutherland had erupted onto the international scene with an amazing performance in Donizetti's *Lucia di Lammermoor*. Attention was shifting elsewhere.

FREELANCE OPERA ENGAGEMENTS

1956

Aug/Sept	Teatro Colón, Buenos Aires	(4)
November	Theatre Royal, Wexford	(4)
		Total: 8

1957

February	Russian Tour	(4)
October	Covent Garden	(4)
November	Covent Garden	(2)
December	Covent Garden	(3)
		Total: 13

1958

January	Covent Garden	(5)
February	Covent Garden	(2)
March	New Theatre, Oxford	(3)
	Palace Theatre, Manchester	(5)
April	Covent Garden	(4)
June	Australian Tour	(4)
July	Australian Tour	(10)
August	Australian Tour	(11)
September	Australian Tour	(7)
October	Australian Tour	(9)
November	Australian Tour	(13)
December	Covent Garden	(2)

Total: 75

1959

January	Covent Garden	(3)
February	Covent Garden	(5)
March	New Theatre, Oxford	(1)
	Palace Theatre, Manchester	(2)
May	Covent Garden	(2)
June	Covent Garden	(1)

Total: 14

1960

September   Covent Garden   (1)
November   Theatre Royal, Liège   (2)

Total: 3

The year 1960 must have been a bitter disappointment for Constance professionally, and it clearly provoked much heart-searching. What of the future? Although opera had always been her first love she might have settled for a diminished career on the concert platform. But here too she was obliged to grapple with uncomfortable facts. For twelve years she had broadcast frequently with the BBC but in 1960, apart from her traditional appearance at the Last Night of the Proms, she was offered no engagements. Even harder to bear must have been the growing indifference of the Hallé programmers and, by inference, of the Hallé conductor Sir John Barbirolli. Ever since mortal illness had laid its hand on Kathleen Ferrier, Constance had been the automatic mezzo/contralto choice for the traditional Easter oratorios at the Free Trade Hall Manchester and the City Hall Sheffield. In 1959 she was invited to perform at Manchester but not at Sheffield. In 1960 she lost both engagements. It was a cruel blow, more especially as she had come to regard Barbirolli, unlike Sargent, as a personal friend. Yet only Sargent – aloof 'Flash Harry' – continued to champion her to the last.

What were her thoughts? She must have wondered if she

was losing her touch or if her voice was beginning to show signs of age. Or was it that her younger contemporaries were simply better than she was? But if that was the case, how was she to account for the unstinted acclaim that she had received in Buenos Aires, Moscow, Berlin? Moreover opera lovers and concert goers were beginning to spring to her defence. The correspondence columns of *Music and Musicians* carried regular letters of protest, of which the following (extract) is a pretty fair sample:

> Instead of ignoring her, Covent Garden should be proud to have available such a gifted English singer. Every encouragement should be given to 'up and coming artists'. But what kind of treatment do some of them get when they have 'arrived'? – (Mrs) Elizabeth E. Mills, S.W.18.

So what was the reason for her sudden eclipse? The answer is almost certainly to be found in that strange, pervasive phenomenon, cultural shift. In plain terms musical taste was changing. Mellowness and sweetness (some would add 'spirituality') were going out of fashion; a certain steeliness or astringency was becoming the order of the day. The signs had been there for some time: in the cold scientific acoustics of the Royal Festival Hall (musical equivalent of the tower block), and in the almost ecstatic acclaim given by musicologists like Walter Legge to the Romanian pianist Dinu Lipatti, whose sensational career was cut tragically short by fatal illness. Lipatti's playing had a clarity and a precision that made one gasp when one first heard it: he seemed to have the fingers of a superman. On closer acquaintance, and if one admired the playing of a pianist like Paderewski, it was possible to feel that Lipatti's technique was not so much superhuman as inhuman: the technique of a digitally-programmed machine. One recalls too the comment of the reviewer at the Bethlehem Bach Festival, who damned with faint praise 'the highly perfumed and polished work' of the Philadelphia Orchestra. Classical oratorio was already moving into the era of 'authentic' performances, with their scaled-down choirs and orchestras and carefully reconstructed 'original' scores (Barbirolli was quick to embrace the mood-change). A new generation of musicians was coming to the fore, anxious to explore and demonstrate a different kind of sound. Constance belonged to the old order. Soul and spirit she was a romantic, with a rich warm voice to match, and it was this, surely, rather than any technical quibbles, that caused her suddenly to lose favour as a concert artist. There is nothing harder to fight against than fashion, especially when it gets elevated to the status of a creed. Yet fashion is, by definition, ephemeral, and the time would come when musicologists would express excitement at the discovery of one or two 'lost' recordings by Constance which were never released commercially. But that was no help to her in 1960.

NOTE : CONSTANCE AS SINGING ACTRESS

This is perhaps an appropriate place to insert one tribute which, above all others, must have given Constance peculiar satisfaction. It belongs to a slightly earlier period of her career but surely stands as the perfect *riposte* to those who have ever claimed that her acting lacked depth or subtlety. Here it is, from one of the greatest Shakespeareans of them all:

Dear Constance Shacklock,

I was at the last night of *Rosenkavalier* and can't let my admiration for your Oktavian go unexpressed. I don't mean to be invidious towards Miss Fisher whom I much admire if I say that next to Lotte Lehmann's Marschallin – and indeed alongside it – will always remain your Oktavian: as a perfect and rare thing, an operatic performance as brilliantly acted as sung. It was, as such rare things always are, a revelation. My most happy gratitude and admiration!

Yours sincerely,

Michael Redgrave.

Bedford House
Chiswick Mall, W4   25th July 1954

Kovlovski congratulates Constance on her performance in *Aida*: Bolshoi Theatre Moscow, 21st February 1957

---

1. *Covent Garden: The Untold Story*, p.185. Quoted from a private interview.

2. Montague Haltrecht, *The Quiet Showman*, p.175.

3. Interview with Jeremy Nicholas, *BBC Radio 3*, 13 September 1996.

4. *Music and Musicians*, May 1957.

5. Taken partly from an article written by Constance for *Music and Musicians*, May 1957, as a companion piece to Joan Hammond's impressions of the tour.

6. See Appendix C.

Dearest Friends —
This foto taken Jan 21. 56 behind Cologne radio station was the very last one of Papet's — I want you to have it as a souvenir. I read and reread your wonderful letter.
Sincerely
Ruth K.

From Ruth Kleiber to Eric and Constance in response to their letter of condolence.

Previous page:

Martha at the Wexford Festival 1956. Constance (Nancy) with Marko Rothmüller (Plunkett)

IX

THE SOUND OF MUSIC

The visit to Liège was Constance's operatic swansong and a not unworthy one. Her performance 'had an unprecedented effect upon the audience' (*La Meuse*). She was 'the true star of the evening, to whom we would offer our admiration' (*Liège Gazette*). 'The part of Azucena is one of the most difficult in the repertoire – the second act is all counter singing and demands sustained care and infallible breath control from the interpreter. Madame Shacklock possesses all the qualities for a great interpretation, full of fire' (*Le Monde du Travail*). 'We have seldom heard an Azucena who could surpass the talent of Madame Shacklock. Her voice, her intense dramatic acting, gained everyone's approval' (*La Wallonie*). The distance between London and Liège is about the same as between London and Newcastle, but there are some distances that can't be measured in miles.

Constance acknowledges that the part of Azucena makes big demands on the singer "both dramatically and vocally. Some of the most intense passages lie in the lower register and one can so easily push the voice. There are occasions when one has to be really disciplined and not let the emotions take over. Dramatically it is a wonderful role to portray and I loved performing it." She also recalls how, many years previously, when she was learning the role at Covent Garden, they were rehearsing the scene from Act

Three in which Azucena is dragged on stage accused of being a witch and has to let out a loud scream. She was informed that she didn't have to do the scream — it would be done by someone in the wings to save her voice. She protested that this was not authentic and that she must do the scream herself. Some time later she learnt to her embarrassment that the scream was normally done by a member of the chorus who was paid an extra seven shillings and sixpence for it. This, as Constance remarks, "was a lot of money in those days and I'm sure she was not pleased at losing it." Nevertheless she dismisses the idea that a scream can damage the voice. After all "as babies we all scream heartily. It's good exercise for the lungs!"

*

The tremendous reception given to Constance at Liège must have worked wonders for her morale. Nevertheless there were difficult decisions to be made. By a strange quirk of fate it so happened that before leaving for Liege she had received a letter from the composer Richard Rodgers (of Rodgers and Hammerstein fame). He had seen her performing at Covent Garden and wondered if she would consider taking the part of the Mother Superior in the forthcoming London production of *The Sound of Music*. It was not what she wanted or hoped for but it *was* stage work, and it offered an unusual way out of her career problem. One is obliged to read between the lines of Constance's autobiographical jottings at this point for she gives no hint of the career crisis that she was then facing — surely a sign that the hurt was deep. She merely remarks that she had no intention of doing a musical "but as he [Richard Rodgers] had written me such a gracious letter I felt that I must be gracious too and see him when he came to London with the producer Terry White and librettist Oscar Hammerstein." The meeting (which included the formality of an audition) was to be at the London Coliseum, and something of the mental turmoil she was then experiencing is suggested by her remark that she was twenty minutes late for the appointment "as I couldn't find anywhere to park, and I thought, Well, that's solved the problem!" However they were still waiting for her when eventually she did arrive. "After many apologies and a chat, I said I would sing 'Softly awakes my heart' from *Samson and Delilah*. When I had finished there was a deadly silence and I wondered what had happened. Then Terry White shouted up from the auditorium in a broad American accent, 'My! With breath control like that you ought to be a deep-sea diver!' " The part was hers – if she wanted it.

"After much thought and a few sleepless nights I decided to accept, thinking it would only be for about six months. Little did I know that it would run for nearly six years! I really felt I had taken the veil because I was completely committed, with eight shows a week. The only day we were not performing was Good Friday. And guess what? – I went to see the film of *The Sound of Music* and loved it. [1] It was a very happy company and we all became good friends."

The big disadvantage of *The Sound of Music* was that it killed what was left of Constance's concert career. She was on stage every night, Monday to Friday, and twice on Saturdays – a gruelling schedule. Nor does it seem that the management was prepared to be flexible in respect of the one really prestigious engagement which was left to her: her hugely popular appearance at the Last Night of the Proms. She sang there in 1961 because she had contracted to do so before accepting the role of the Mother Superior (an insert in that night's programme for *The Sound of Music* apologized for her absence and explained why). But she was not allowed to do so in either 1962 or 1963, and her very last appearance at the Proms, in 1964, seems to have been the result of some pretty strenuous representations – presumably from Sir Malcolm Sargent, backed up by the BBC. Contractual inflexibility was a high price to pay for her involvement in *The Sound of Music*, and it reveals a less than pleasant side to what popular imagination likes to think of as 'the happy musical'.

Nevertheless there were many compensations. In December 1961 the BBC made a recording of Constance singing 'Climb every mountain', and thanks to its almost daily repetition on the *Light Programme* it was soon known and loved all over Britain. Thousands of Nottingham folk made the journey to London in hired coaches to see and hear their now celebrated local singer, and many of them were introduced to Constance and taken backstage by her. Those who were thus favoured and who are still alive, talk of her great warmth and friendliness, usually adding that it was one of the highlights of their life. Occasionally too the show had a therapeutic effect on some distressed individual. "A young man on the point of committing suicide was coming along Shaftsbury Avenue towards Cambridge Circus when he saw the name of the show in bright lights over the front of the Palace Theatre. [2] He said that something compelled him to walk in. Usually the performance was sold out but on this occasion there was one ticket left. Thereafter he never looked back. He saw the show over two hundred times.

"Also, a young mother, who had lost her young child very tragically, withdrew completely into herself and couldn't bear to go anywhere where there were young children. Her family greatly feared for her but eventually persuaded her to come to *The Sound of Music*. I was told she cried for three days almost non-stop, but it was the start of her recovery. I'm sure there were many more healings during the six years but these are ones I know about. I have no regrets at doing a musical. It reached many thousands of people who would never go to the opera and the music by Richard Rodgers was so lovely." Constance remarks on the pleasure it gave her to hear their paper boy whistling its tunes.

Then, quite suddenly, in March 1965, Eric died of a heart attack. Constance passes quickly over her bereavement, simply remarking that she was away from the show for ten days and that the company were "just marvellous to me. It was their love and kindness that helped me to continue performing." Letters of condolence poured in: from Covent Garden, from distinguished musicians, some of whom had worked closely with Eric and were anxious to pay tribute to his remarkable talents, and from their many friends. Constance kept them all.

How much she missed Eric may be gauged from her frequent affectionate references to him in her writings, from his skill and patience in coaching her in so many of her roles, and from his own self-effacing role as her increasingly regular accompanist. It had, in truth, been a musical partnership as well as an extraordinarily happy marriage. Had she been still at Covent Garden she would probably have retired almost immediately – the place held too many memories. As it was she carried on for the duration of the show, finding consolation and distraction in the work. For her too, *The Sound of Music* was evidently therapeutic.

"By the end of the run [one year later] I had come to terms with myself. I did a few concerts after the show finished but I felt strongly that now was the time to retire. Dear Eric always said, 'Give up while people remember you, Constance. Don't go on and fade out.' This I now decided to do, and to give my final recital at the little church in Bulwell where I sang my first solo. However it became very clear that the church would not hold the number of people wanting to come and so it was transferred to the main church in town (3). It was a very moving occasion but also very exciting. When I arrived to find mounted police controlling the traffic, may I be forgiven for purring loudly? My programme consisted of items representing all the varied music I had sung over the years: operatic arias, well-known ballads, oratorio excerpts, finishing with 'Rule Britannia!' accompanied by the Nottingham Male Voice Choir. I was very deeply moved by the standing ovation I received, but deeply grateful that I had been able to use my gifts to give pleasure to so many people.

"So this was the end of my performing career."

---

1. This of course was later. The film version (with Julie Andrews) was released in 1965.

2. Few people realise that the Palace Theatre was built by Richard D'Oyly Carte as an opera house. Sullivan's only grand opera *Ivanhoe* was performed there.

3. The parish church of St Mary and All Souls, Bulwell.

4. After this sentence comes a section break. Later however, Constance added in handwriting at this point, three paired memories:

"Two treasured career memories: my time at Covent Garden, and the Last Night of the Proms, where I sang 'Rule Britannia!' ten times under Sir Malcolm Sargent.

"My two favourite oratorios: *Gerontius* and the Verdi *Requiem*.

"My two favourite operas: *Tristan und Isolde* and *Der Rosenkavalier*. *Tristan* because of my treasured memories of Kirsten Flagstad and dear Eric who coached me in the part of Brangäne; *Rosenkavalier* for memories of Erich Kleiber who I called my Fairy Godfather."

X

AFTERWARDS

"How long the days at home seemed to be! I had been out every evening for six years and now time seemed to stand still. I started to do some new tapestries for my dining room chairs and piano stool. This kept me occupied but it didn't fill the psychological void. I felt so lonely. What should I do next? I couldn't just sit around, whiling away the hours. One morning in June I was feeling particularly desolate and pondering what life was all about when it came to me so clearly: You've had a wonderful career. You have been privileged to work with some of the world's greatest singers and musicians. You must now pass on your knowledge to a new generation. I had never thought of teaching. However the idea wouldn't go away and I began to wonder what should be my first move. I decided to ring up my old college and speak to Sir Thomas Armstrong, who knew me through my career and was now Principal of the RAM. Fortunately he was in his office when I phoned and we had a chat about the possibility of my becoming a professor there. He asked me what I was doing for lunch. 'Why not come and dine with me at the RAM?' I did so, and we talked, finding so much in common. Time just slipped away. It ended with my being offered a professorship for the following September (1967). At 9 o'clock that morning I had been wondering what to do with my life! When I arrived home at 4 p.m. my future was very clearly mapped out.

"That first term I had five students. I must admit that on the first morning I was very nervous, and when a shy young Irish boy appeared and told me that he was a counter-tenor I felt really troubled. How on earth would I train a counter-tenor? I asked him to sing some songs and, to my great surprise, he chose three which had been part of my own repertoire. What was even stranger, the notes which I had found difficult, he had difficulty with too. I began to relax – here was a meeting point. We worked very well together for about three years, after which he became a chorister in the Chapel Royal at Windsor.

"I grew very fond of my students. They became almost like family and it gave me great joy to see them developing and fulfilling themselves. I was Professor there for sixteen years and I found the work very rewarding. I had good voices to guide and my students were lovely young people. Even now I get Christmas cards from many of them, telling me what they are doing with their lives. After I left the RAM I continued teaching privately at home. I have a large music room, completely detached, so that one is free to make as much sound as in a performance without disturbing anyone. I always feel grateful that I don't have to turn out when the weather is bad!

"It was while I was teaching at the RAM that I was asked to hear a singer from Birmingham who was well known for her performances with the Birmingham Operatic Society. Her name was Jean Tredaway and she was a draughtswoman by profession. I was greatly impressed with her beautiful mezzo voice and asked her if she would like to study regularly with me, which she did. One day, when we had been working on the part of the Angel in *Gerontius*, I had such a strong feeling that she ought to be in the profession that I told her so. Imagine my surprise when she replied that she would give up her job if there were any possible chance. The result was an audition at Covent Garden and the offer of a place in the chorus. Great excitement! Then came the problem of finding somewhere for her to live. I remember saying to her, 'You can stay with me for three weeks while you search for suitable accommodation in London.' That was in 1971 and she has been with me ever since. I say jokingly that she is still looking!"

Jean was a very special case. Increasingly she filled the place of the daughter that Constance never had and eventually Constance adopted her. But it illustrates a general point: for Constance, teaching was a matter of personal relationships. Only by getting to know one's students, she believed, could one bring out the very best in them. If they travelled from the provinces for a lesson she would lay on lunch; and if there was a problem in getting back home she would offer a bed for the night. She also saw the learning process as something which involved the whole person. Another student, who at first made rapid progress, suddenly seemed unable to get any further. Constance divined that there was a deep-seated personal problem and persuaded her to talk about it. 'The profound change this brought about in my life was mirrored in the development of my voice,' the student later wrote. She added, 'When I am asked what I will remember most of Constance I would say, her warmth, her laughter, her love of animals, her generosity, and most of all her friendship. It is not only that she was a great teacher of singing. I miss the small things: the cosy lunches she made, the sandwiches and cups of tea we shared, and the packed supper she insisted on making me for my journey home. They were very real signs that she cared.' [1]

Constance's capacity for laughter could triumph even over grief. Shortly after she retired from the RAM her mother died at the age of 92. "She had only been living with us for a few months but we shall never forget her passing. The doctor who attended her and who signed the death certificate explained that since it was to be a cremation we must have the signature of another doctor, and that he had arranged for one to call on us at about eleven-thirty a.m. Round about that time there was a knock on the door and I opened it to see a very charming, elegant-looking gentleman standing there. Before he had a chance to explain who he was I said, 'Good morning. Do come in. I'm Constance, Mrs Shacklock's daughter,' and took him to the small room where Mother was lying. He took one look at her and went quite pale. 'But Madam,' he protested. 'I'm from Allied Carpets and I've come to measure the attic!'

Between tears and convulsive laughter, and with the carpet man muttering, 'My wife won't believe this,' Constance and her sister Rosamund hurried him away, tendering their apologies. "The fact is that about two months previously I had decided to recarpet the attic, but with all the business of nursing Mother it had completely slipped my mind. I'm sure the story was related very often by the Allied Carpets man."

Some years later, Constance paid a second visit to the Soviet Union and this time it was Rosamund who accompanied her. When Constance was on tour there, in 1957, she had been asked to do extra concerts and make television appearances but could not be paid in English currency. The roubles that she earned were paid into a Moscow bank account in her name but because of currency restrictions could not be taken out of the country. Many years later, in 1988, she learned that the original conversion rate of her bank balance had been £10,000! However in 1962 the rouble had been devalued, leaving her with just £1000 in sterling equivalent. She was now able to withdraw this by letter from the bank in Moscow, but discovered that there was still £800 interest remaining which the bank could not transfer. The thought came to her: why not take a holiday?

"My sister Rosamund was celebrating her 70th birthday and I felt it would be a lovely idea to take her to Russia. She was thrilled at the prospect and I started to make enquiries. I was told I would have to book through a travel agency which would only accept English currency, not Russian, and that the booking had to be done over here. The idea came to me to write to the British Ambassador out there, Sir Roderick Braithwaite, and explain the situation, asking if there were any hotels where we could book privately. Imagine my surprise and joy when he wrote back and said

ABOVE: Constance with her mother and sister Rosamund, February 1960 (photo: London News Agency). BELOW: Constance and Jean Tredaway, 1978

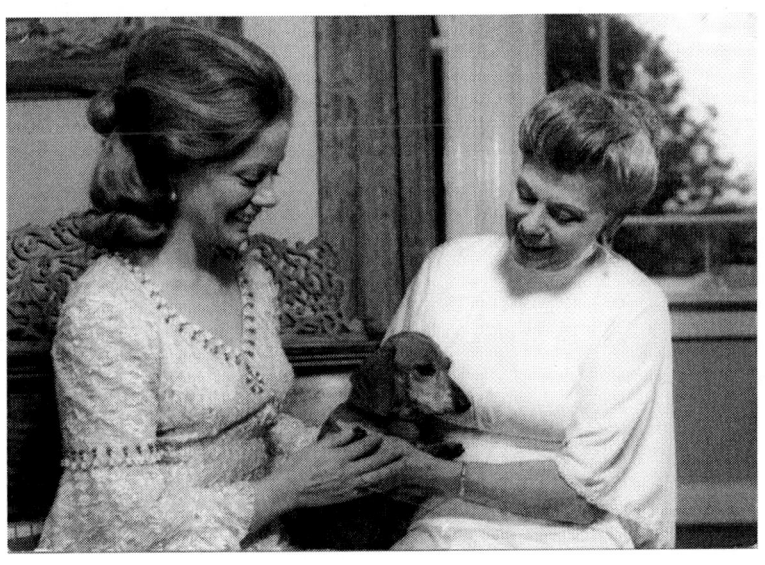

that he was the son of Warwick Braithwaite, a conductor at Covent Garden, and that he had been taken to a performance of *Der Rosenkavalier* conducted by his father, in which I had sung Octavian. He added that he and his wife would be delighted to entertain my sister and me for a week's stay."

So began the unique brief adventure of Constance's later years. The Soviet Union as it was still officially called was then in the middle years of the Gorbachev era. *Glasnost* was dissolving the old barriers and rigidities, and the map of Europe was about to be redrawn. More obviously the Soviet economy was beginning to show signs of terminal breakdown. "Everything was terribly expensive. A little T-shirt which would have been £3 at home was the equivalent of £27. No wonder there was so much poverty around. Our chauffeur, Constantine, who took us around the Embassy's Rolls Royce, which was at our disposal for the whole week, asked us if we would like to have a meal with him and his wife. Of course we were delighted. His home was in a building something like a block of council flats but with no light in the entrance, and a terrifying lift, so old and rickety that we were gratefully relieved when we reached Constantine's floor. His flat was one room which they had sub-divided with a wooden panel to enable them and their two teenage sons to have a little privacy. It had a tiny kitchen, and a bathroom into which one could only just squeeze. They told us they now had enough money for a larger flat but could not move unless someone was prepared to make an exchange as all properties belonged to the State. Constantine had been a stunt driver for films before his retirement and considered himself very lucky to have obtained his present job with the British Embassy. He and his wife, a teacher, had gone to so much trouble to welcome us. They gave us a memorable meal and there were special drinks in our honour. We felt very privileged to have visited their home and their kindness to us will not be forgotten."

Of course there was much sight-seeing to be done but for Constance, the highlight of the week was a visit to the celebrated Moscow State Circus. She recalls some breathtaking feats by trapeze artists ("Constantine remarked that there was no room for error – just like being a stunt driver") and a remarkable display of ice-skating. "Then came the wonder of the evening: three large white polar bears came skating in. We just held our breaths to see these huge creatures with ice-skates fastened to their back legs and standing upright, performing incredible feats with their trainer. They seemed to be really enjoying it, especially when they were given an uproarious ovation. I love all animals but I must admit I was glad a safety net had been erected before they performed as at times they were only three feet away from us.

"As we neared the end of that wonderful week the thought kept coming to me: how was I going to spend the £800 that had been banked there since 1957? The only thing of any value was a picture, but as I have many pictures in my home I felt this would not be spending the money wisely. Then Lady Braithwaite rather tentatively came up with a thought which she said she would not be offended if I rejected. Twelve nuns were themselves rebuilding their convent which had been desecrated during the Stalin regime. Would I consider giving the money to help them. This seemed to me such a very right idea. So somewhere in Moscow I have a few bricks of love in a Russian convent."

*

When Constance returned from Moscow she was in her 76th year and beginning to age gracefully. At one time she had threatened to grow stout, and Kleiber, for one, had begun to be anxious about her weight, fearing the effect it would have on her role as the youthful Octavian. 'Papito and I are delighted that you are coming to the Colón this season and we shall be very proud of you I know,' Kleiber's wife Ruth wrote to her at the beginning of 1956. 'Your German was so marvellous in Brangäne that you will surely learn the Oktavian easily. Papito says please not to get fat and to *look* (underlined), play and sing as you did in London.' A charming and delicate way of putting it! On the other hand, the portly figure who sang 'Rule Britannia!' in those last few performances at the Proms looked every inch the part ('commanding presence and voice to match' as Alan Blyth recalls in the *Dictionary of National Biography*). With the passing of time however, Constance had grown thinner, though her voice remained richly musical and her energy seemed undiminished. For many years she had lived at Kingston-on-Thames and in 1985 she had been invited to become President of the annual four-weekly Kingston May Arts Festival, a role into which she threw herself with her usual zest. "A lot of work goes into its organization but

Constance and Jean, 1991 (photo: Mike Jones)

it gives so much pleasure and is now well-known throughout the country," she remarked. In 1993 she received an honorary doctorate from Kingston University and in 1995 she became Life President of the Association of Teachers of Singing. In 1971 she had been awarded the OBE, and a move to honour her with the title DBE was in progress at the time of her death. One can only regret that it didn't come a little sooner for it would have set the seal on her life.

At the very beginning of 1999 Constance began to feel unwell and found herself increasingly unable to eat. True to her philosophy as a Christian Scientist she made light of the matter and refused to seek medical aid. In all probability it made little difference for she was suffering from cancer of the pancreas which by that time was almost certainly terminal. She was still driving her car, giving private lessons and displaying her customary cheerfulness at the beginning of June, but a few days later she had to admit that she was too ill to leave the house. In retrospect it seems amazing that she continued to live an outwardly normal life for so long. She died, still at her home in Kingston Vale, on June 29th. She was 86. Among the many tributes and letters of condolence which Jean received was one from a well-known West End producer who had ventured to write to Constance when he was a struggling drama student, hardly daring to hope for a reply. 'Her encouragement and advice gave me the determination to aim for things I believed were beyond me,' he wrote. Another, from Norman Lebrecht, concluded: 'I think it can be safely said that she did not have a bad word for anyone.'

It was inevitable that there should be a memorial service for Constance. Actually there were three, but the main one, attended by the good and the great, and by very many people whose lives had been altered by her kindly influence, took place on 19 March 2000, in St Paul's Church, Covent Garden. It was the obvious venue. Moreover by an extraordinarily happy coincidence it was in this church that Thomas Arne, the composer of 'Rule Britannia!' had been baptized in 1710, and laid to rest in 1778.

But then, perhaps what we call 'coincidence' is merely the inscrutable logic of History.

1. From a Nottingham church newsletter. Sept 1999

APPENDIX A

Opera roles, with year of first appearance, and number of appearances in the role.

1946

The Fairy Queen (Mystery, Summer, Votaress)	34

1947

Carmen (Mercedes)	19
Manon (Rosette)	13
The Magic Flute (3rd Lady)	35
Der Rosenkavalier (Annina)	26
Carmen (Carmen)	110
Peter Grimes (Mrs Sedley)	18
Il Trovatore (Azucena)	10

1948

Die Meistersinger (Magdalene)	25
Tristan und Isolde (Brangäne)	45
Die Walküre (Grimgerde)	33
Boris Godunov (Marina)	23
Der Rosenkavalier (Octavian)	71

1949

Aida (Amneris)	100
Götterdämmerung (1st Norn; Flosshilde)	6
Salome (Herodias)	13

1950

Das Rheingold (Fricka) — 1

Die Walküre (Fricka) — 1

1952

The Marriage of Figaro (Cherubino) — 1

1953

Gloriana (Queen Elizabeth) — 4

Lohengrin (Ortrud) — 24

1954

Electra (3rd Maid) — 2

Das Rheingold (Erda) — 2

Siegfried (Erda) — 2

Götterdämmerung (2nd Norn) — 11

1955

Tales of Hoffman (Voice of the Mother) — 8

1956

Martha (Nancy) — 4

GRAND TOTAL — **641**

APPENDIX B

RECITALS AND CONCERT APPEARANCES

Constance gave recitals and made occasional broadcasts from the time when she was a student but apart from four CEMA recitals she seems never to have kept a list of them. It was Eric who began to record her professional engagements, commencing about a month before they were married. The details are contained in two foolscap-sized ledgers, with the opera engagements listed separately at the back of ledger 1. For some curious reason he did not record her substitute performances – ie. where she stood in at short notice for the regular singer – and after his death in March 1965 the entries cease. By that time however Constance was fully occupied with *The Sound of Music* and seems to have made only one or two further appearances on the concert platform.

Eric's ledgers are thus very valuable documents and record her engagements for a period of eighteen years in great detail. Every recital is fully itemized and after 20 February 1951 her concert fees are also listed. Eric even mentions what dress she wore and the name of the agency if one was employed.

The following is an abridged summary of all her concert appearances and recitals as recorded in the ledgers together with her very last platform appearance. RAH = Royal Albert Hall; RFH = Royal Festival Hall; HWPC = Henry Wood Promenade Concert; A = Accompanist; Some orchestra initials need no explanation but less familiar initials refer as follows: BBCCO = BBC Concert Orchestra; BBCOO = BBC Opera Orchestra;

BBCTO = BBC Theatre Orchestra; BPO = Berlin Philharmonic Orchestra; BMO = Bournemouth Municipal Orchestra, subsequently BSO, the Bournemouth Symphony Orchestra; CGO = Covent Garden Orchestra; PO = Philharmonia Orchestra; REO = Radio Eireann Orchestra; SNO = Scottish National Orchestra; WNO = Welsh National Orchestra; YSO = Yorkshire Symphony Orchestra (conceived as a front-rank orchestra to serve particularly the industrial towns and cities of the West Riding excluding Sheffield. Unfortunately council cut-backs led to its early demise). The BBC regional orchestras (long defunct) are denoted thus: BBCMLO = BBC Midland Light Orchestra; BBCNO = BBC Northern Orchestra; BBC Scot = BBC Scottish Orchestra; BBCWO = BBC Welsh Orchestra. Where an orchestra was involved the name is that of the Conductor.

* denotes broadcast performance.

1948		
21/6	Bournemouth	Recital
4/7	Maida Vale Studios*	Mozart *Requiem* RPO Beecham
5/7	Maida Vale Studios*	(repeat of above)
14/8	Buxton	Recital
15/8	Buxton	Two Recitals (afternoon and
16/8	RAH HWPC	Wagner item LSO Basil
30/8	RAH HWPC	Wagner item LSO Basil Cameron
15/10	Camden Theatre*	Concert BBC Theatre Orchestra Clifton Helliwell

27/11	Leeds	Recital
4/12	Harrogate	Recital
5/12	Cricklewood	Recital A: Cyril Weller
18/12	Durham Cath.	Messiah Conrad Eden
1949		
2/1	Southend	Concert CGO Warwick Braithwaite
8/1	BBC TV*	Scene from *Carmen* with Edgar Evans. Eric Robinson
19/1	Bridgend	Recital A: Alan Richardson
22/1	Central Hall Westminster	Gounod *Faust* (concert version) Allan Brown
30/1	Leeds	Recital A: Clifton Helliwell
31/1	Harrogate	(repeat of above)
2/2	Nottingham	(repeat of above)
3/3	Swansea	Recital A: Clifton Helliwell
13/3	Colne	Recital A: Margaret Gott
15/4	Manchester*	Stanford *Stabat Mater* BBCNO Charles Groves
28/4	Dorchester Hotel	Concert (Monteverdi item) Walter Goehr
22/5	RAH	Verdi *Requiem* Reginald Jacques
2/6	RAH	Verdi *Requiem* Victor de Sabata
5/6	EMI Studios	Tristan (recorded excerpt) PO Karl Bohm
24/6	Exmouth	Concert
11/7	Dudley	Concert (Programme A) ROH Chorus tour

12/7	Leicester	Concert (Programme A)
13/7	Wolverhampton	Concert (Programme A)
14/7	Leicester	Concert (Programme B)
15/7	Nottingham	Concert (Programme A)
17/7	Birmingham	Concert (Programme A)
18/7	Ferndale	Concert (Programme B)
19/7	Bristol	Concert (Programme A)
20/7	Newport	Concert (Programme B)
21/7	Cheltenham	Concert (Programme A &B)
22/7	Bristol	Concert (Programme B)
23/7	Newport	Concert (Programme A)
24/7	Cardiff	Concert (Programme B)
25/7	Wimbledon	Concert (Programme B)
3/9	Buxton	Recital
4/9	Buxton	Recital
8/9	Hampton Court	Blow: *Venus and Adonis* Anthony Lewis
9/9	Hampton Court*	(repeat of above)
10/9	Hampton Court	(repeat of above)
11/9	Ashington	Recital
21/9	BBC Broadcast*	Strauss Recital A: Frederick Stone
2/10	Colne	Recital A: Margaret Gott
22/10	BBC Broadcast*	Verdi *Requiem* BBCSO Rafael Kubelik
23/10	BBC Broadcast*	(repeat performance)
5/11	Sheffield	Verdi *Requiem* Halle Barbirolli
6/11	Manchester	(repeat of above)

20/11	RAH	*Choral Symphony* LPO Nikolai Malko
20/12	RAH	*Messiah* LPO Frederic Jackson
1950		
7/1	Brighton	*Messiah* LPO Frederic Jackson
14/1	RAH	Promenade Concert LPO Basil Cameron
21/1	BBC Broadcast*	Vivaldi *Juditha Triumphans* PO Trevor Harvey
1/2	BBC Broadcast*	(repeat of above)
5/2	Southend	Concert items PO Walter Goehr
9/2	RAH	Beethoven *Missa Solemnis* LPO Eduard Van Beinum
11/2	Wigmore Hall	Janacek *Diary of One Who Disappeared* A: John Wills
2/3	BBC Broadcast*	Liszt *St Elizabeth* BBCSO Sir Adrian Boult
26/3	RAH	Bach *St John Passion* Reginald Jacques
9/4	Ferndale	Recital (no details)
29/4	Redhill	Concert items Reginald Jacques
3/5	Mansfield	Gluck *Orpheo* (concert version)
13/5	Swansea	Dvorak *Stabat Mater* Gwylim Roberts
14/5	Aberdare	Concert items
24/5	St Margaret's Westminster	Vaughan Williams *Magnificat* John Tobin

18/7	BBC Broadcast*	*Il Trovatore* (extracts) Opera Orch. Clifton Helliwell
20/7	BBC Broadcast*	(repeat of above)
29/7	Neath	*Messiah* and Verdi *Requiem* extracts
14/8	RAH HWPC	Wagner item LPO Basil Cameron
16/9	RAH HWPC*	Last Night of the Proms BBCSO Sargent
17/9	BBC Birmingham*	Two arias BBCMLO Gilbert Vintner
23/9	Swansea	Elgar The Music Makers LPO Sir Adrian Boult
24/9	Merthyr Tydfil	Concert items
30/9	Ealing	Short recital
8/10	Colne	Concert items
18/10	Middlesborough	Recital (with Nowakowski)
29/10	Aberdare	Recital (with George James) A: Anne Walker
3/11	RAM	Short recital A: Eric Mitchell
15/11	Leeds	Verdi *Requiem* YSO Sir Malcolm Sargent
21/11	Birmingham	Verdi *Requiem* CBSO David Willcocks
2/12	Central Hall Westminster	*Messiah* Allan Brown
9/12	Sheffield	*Messiah* CBSO Herbert Bardgett
12/12	BBC Birmingham*	Two songs by Saint-Saëns BBCMLO Vintner

17/12	Bournemouth	Concert items BMO
31/12	Hanley	*Messiah*
1951		
9/1	BBC Birmingham*	*Carmen* items BBCMLO Gilbert Vintner
11/1	Leicester	Recital A: Hubert Greenslade
16/1	Central Hall, Westminster	Concert items A: Eric Mitchell; Harold Rawlinson
3/2	Epsom College	Recital A: Eric Mitchell
11/2	Maida Vale Studios*	Vivaldi *Juditha Triumphans* Trevor Harvey
13/2	Maida Vale Studios*	(Repeat performance)
17/2	Liverpool	*Israel in Egypt* Liv.PO Sir Malcolm Sargent
19/2	Camden Theatre*	*Diary of One Who Disappeared* A: Walter Susskind
24/2	Central Hall, Westminster	*Rosenkavalier* items (R. Meyer Children's concert)
25/2	Llanelly	Concert items
16/3	Troon	Recital A: Eric Mitchell
20/3	Nottingham	Recital A: Eric Mitchell
11/4	BBC London*	Mozart items Karl Haas
15/4	Glasgow	*Carmen* (Concert version) SNO Walter Susskind
19/4	BBC Cardiff*	Operatic concert BBCWO Rae Jenkins
24/4	BBC London*	RPS Centenary Concert RPO Sir Thomas Beecham

3/5	Neath	Handel *Israel in Egypt*
13/5	Blackpool	Concert items A: Eric Mitchell
15/5	Rowton Castle	Recital A: Eric Mitchell
22/5	BBC London*	*Aida* excerpts BBCOO Stanford Robinson
24/5	BBC London*	(repeat performance)
6/6	BBC Birmingham*	*Carmen* items
10/6	Bournemouth	Beethoven *Mass in D* BMO Rudolph Schwarz
13/6	Salisbury Cathedral	(repeat of above)
14/6	Bournemouth	*Das Lied von der Erde* BMO Rudolph Schwarz
21/6	RFH	Recital (items) A: Eric Mitchell
8/7	BBC London*	Concert items BBCOO Stanford Robinson
8/8	Llanwrst	Dvorak *Stabat Mater*
23/9	Buxton	Concert items William Rees
29/9	Wigan	Concert items
6/10	Swindon	Concert items
28/10	Aberdare	Recital (with others) A: Eric Mitchell
11/11	Radio Hilversum*	Bellini *Norma* (concert version) Willem Lohoff
17/11	Mexborough	*Messiah*
1/12	Worksop College	Concert items

1952			
5/1	BBC Cardiff*	Two songs BBCWO Arwel Hughes	
12/1	BBC London*	Schoenberg *Gurrelieder* RPO Karl Rankl	
13/1	BBC London*	(repeat performance)	
23/1	Swindon	Recital A: Eric Mitchell	
7/2	Halifax	Concert items	
24/2	Bulwell	Organ & vocal recital with Eric Mitchell	
6/3	Ruthin	Recital A: Eric Mitchell	
9/3	New Mills	Concert items	
16/3	Radio	Opera concert Willem Lohoff	
20/3	Hanley	*Aida* (concert version) Sir Malcolm Sargent	
22/3	RAH	(repeat of the above)	
20/3	Manchester	*Aida* -Act 2 (concert) Halle Sir John Barbirolli	
30/3	Manchester	(repeat performance)	
2/4	BBC Midland*	Two arias BBCMLO Gilbert Vintner	
23/4	Paisley	Concert items Allan Craig	
3/5	Liverpool	*Aida* (concert version) Sir Malcolm Sargent	
17/5	Leeds	Three arias YSO Maurice Miles	
19/5	ROH	Beethoven *Choral Symphony* ROHO Erich Kleiber	

20/7	Buxton	Concert items
4/8	RAH HWPC	Aria BBCSO Sir Malcolm Sargent
19/8	BBC Cardiff*	Three items BBCWO Arwel Hughes
4/9	RAH HWPC	Wagner item BBCSO Sir Malcolm Sargent
6/9	Nottingham	Concert items A: Eric Mitchell
13/9	RAH HWPC	*Aida* excerpt BBCSO Sir Malcolm Sargent
18/9	Brecon Cathedral	Concert items Rae Jenkins
28/9	Bournemouth	Concert items BMO Charles Groves
5/10	Nottingham	Concert items A: Eric Mitchell
9/10	Maria Grey Training Coll	Lecture with songs
15/10	Middlesborough	Concert items A: Gavin Kay
26/10	Colne	Concert items A: Margaret Gott
30/11	BBC Cardiff*	Three items WNO Rae Jenkins
14/12	Burnley	Concert items A: Ernest Lush
1953		
22/1	BBC London*	Haydn *The Return of Tobias* BBCSO Sargent
31/1	Leeds	*Carmen* excerpts
8/2	ROH	Recital A: Eric Mitchell

4/3	BBC Glasgow*	Elgar *Sea Pictures* BBC Scot Alexander Gibson
7/3	Liverpool	Verdi *Requiem* PO Hugo Rignold
22/3	Manchester	Opera concert Halle Sir John Barbirolli
2/4	Manchester	Elgar *Gerontius* Halle Sir John Barbirolli
4/4	Sheffield	(repeat of above)
5/4	Aberdare	Concert items
5/5	BBC Manchester*	De Falla *El Amor Brujo* BBCNO John Hopkins
27/5	Harrogate	Elgar *Sea Pictures* Halle Sir John Barbirolli
7/6	Birmingham	Haydn *Coronation Mass* CBSO David Willcocks
16/9	Walthamstow	*Messiah* recording (Nixa) LSO Hermann Scherchen
17/9		(continuation of above)
18/9		(continuation of above)
19/9		(continuation of above)
19/9	RAH HWPC*	Last Night of the Proms BBCSO Sargent
26/9	Birmingham	Recital A: Eric Mitchell
11/10	BBC Manchester*	De Falla *El Amor Brujo* BBCNO John Hopkins
17/10	Swansea	*Aida* (concert version) LPO John Pritchard
24/10	RAH	Elgar *The Kingdom* LSO Sir Malcolm Sargent

31/10	Liverpool	*Aida* (concert version) Sir Malcolm Sargent
.1/11	Birmingham	*Aida* (concert version) CBSO Sir Malcolm Sargent
.8/11	BBC London*	Arias Peter Gellhorn
14/11	BBC Midland*	Concert items BBCMLO Gilbert Vintner
18/11	Huddersfield	Brahms *Alto Rhapsody*
29/11	Burnley	(no details)
5/12	Sheffield	*Messiah* Halle
12/12	Sheffield	*Messiah* Halle
13/12	Manchester	(repeat of above)
1954		
8/1	Porth	Concert items Stanley Williams
20/1	Nantyglo	*Aida* (concert version) Elvet Meyrick
21/1	Nantyglo	(repeat performance)
17/2	Paisley	Concert items A: James Breingan; Allan Craig
7/3	Rawtenstall	Concert items A: Herbert Fox
27/3	Nottingham	Elgar *Gerontius* Herbert Bardgett
3/4	Newcastle Cathedral	Verdi *Requiem* Kenneth F. Malcolmson
11/4	Nottingham	Concert items A: Eric Mitchell
15/4	Manchester	Elgar *Gerontius* Halle Sir John Barbirolli

18/4	Manchester	*Messiah* Halle Sir John Barbirolli
1/5	BBC Birmingham*	Concert items BBCMLO Gilbert Vintner
5/5	Brierley Hill	*Carmen* (concert version)
8/5	Liverpool	*Meistersinger* excerpts Stanford Robinson
13/5	Newtown	Verdi *Requiem* Halle Sir John Barbirolli
20/6	Bournemouth	Concert items BSO Charles Groves
25/8	Edinburgh	Schoenberg *Gurrelieder* SNO Karl Rankl
26/8	RAH HWPC	*Tristan* – Act 2 Halle Sir John Barbirolli
4/9	Edinburgh	Verdi Requiem Halle Sir John Barbirolli
18/9	RAH HWPC*	Last Night of the Proms BBCSO Sargent
26/9	Dublin	Elgar *Gerontius* Milan Horvat
3/10	Buxton	*Trovatore* excerpts A: Doris Lester; Wm Rees
31/10	Sutton-in-Ashfield	Concert items
30/11	Birmingham	Aida (concert version) CBSO
5/12	BBC London*	Aria Vic Oliver
11/12	Sheffield	*Messiah* Halle Sir John Barbirolli
12/12	Manchester	(repeat of above)
22/12	Sheffield	*Messiah* Halle Sir John Barbirolli

1955		
2/1	BBC London*	3 items (Grand Hotel)
9/1	RAH	Verdi *Requiem* BBSO Sir Malcolm Sargent
16/1	Sutton Coldfield	Recital A: Eric Mitchell
30/1	Kirkaldy	Concert items A: Isobel Forsyth; John Faulds
2/2	Glasgow	Recital items
3/2	Glasgow	(repeat of above)
9/2	Nottingham	Concert items
16/2	Plymouth	Saint-Saëns *Samson & Delilah* (concert version)
1/3	Colne	Concert items A: Margaret Gott; John Parkinson
5/3	Sheffield	Verdi *Requiem* Halle Sir John Barbirolli
12/3	Liverpool	Verdi *Requiem* Liv PO Sir Malcolm Sargent
26/3	RAH	*Aida* (concert version) BBCSO Sargent
2/4	Sheffield	Elgar *Gerontius* Halle Sir John Barbirolli
7/4	Manchester	(repeat of above)
10/4	Manchester	*Messiah* Halle Sir John Barbirolli
21/4	Tonypandy	Concert items
31/5	BBC London*	Concert items BBCCO Charles Mackerras

2/6	HMV Recording	Gay *The Beggar's Opera* Sir Malcolm Sargent
3/6	HMV Recording	(continuation of above)
4/6	HMV Recording	(continuation of above)
5/6	HMV Recording	(continuation of above)
6/6	HMV Recording	(continuation of above)
16/6	Holy Trinity SW7	Recital items Organ: Stanley Stubbs
25/6	Glasgow	Opera concert SNO Karl Rankl
30/6	Herne Bay	Concert items
5/9	Hereford Cathedral	Verdi *Requiem* Meredith Davies
16/9	BBC London*	Interview with Sydney Harrison
17/9	RAH HWPC*	Last Night of the Proms BBCSO Sargent
20/9	ROH*	BBC recording CGO Reginald Goodall
22/9	ROH*	BBC recording CGO Warwick Braithwaite
30/9	Ruthin	Recital A: Eric Mitchell
1/10	Wigan	*Carmen* (concert version) J.W. Johnson
2/10	Colwyn Bay	Concert items Charles Haberreiter
17/10	Assoc. Rediffusion*	*Land of Hope and Glory* (TV transmission)
18/10	Oldham	Elgar *The Music Makers* Frank Berry

22/10	RAH	Handel *Solomon* LSO Sir Malcolm Sargent
23/10	Marple	Recital A: Eric Mitchell
4/11	Huddersfield	Verdi *Requiem* Liv PO Sir Malcolm Sargent
13/11	St Pancras Town Hall	Charity concert
17/11	Newport	Recital A: Eric Mitchell
23/11	Plymouth	*Aida* (concert version)
10/12	Sheffield	*Messiah* Halle Sir John Barbirolli
11/12	Manchester	(repeat of above)
15/12	Halifax	Works concert A: Shackleton Pollard
1956		
14/1	Worthing	Joint recital A: Wilfred Parry
18/1	Croydon	*Rule Britannia* (Magna Carta Society) A: Eric Mitchell
6/2	Grosvenor House	Concert items (Company dinner) A: Eric Mitchell
8/2	Chester	Recital (no details) A: Eric Mitchell
16/2	Neath	Concert items A: Jeannie Reddin
4/3	BBC London*	Beethoven *Choral Symphony* BBCSO Sargent

25/3	BBC Birmingham*	Arias (TV Concert Hour) BBCMLO Gilbert Vintner
29/3	RFH	Verdi *Requiem* LSO Sir Malcolm Sargent
7/4	RAH	*Land of Hope and Glory* Halle Sir John Barbirolli (RAF Benevolent Fund concert in the presence of the Queen & the Duke of Edinburgh)
20/4	BBC London*	Two items (TV concert)
22/4	Kensington	Recital A: Eric Mitchell (Society for Cultural Relations with the USSR)
24/4	RFH	Beethoven *Choral Symphony* PO Stanley Pope
2/5	Dudley	Verdi *Requiem* Graham Price
10/5	Newtown	*Messiah* Halle Sir John Barbirolli
24/5	Sheffield	Concert items Halle Hermann Linders
10/6	Pontypridd	Concert items A: Edward Downes
17/6	BBC London*	Three items (Grand Hotel)
1/7	Colwyn Bay	Concert items Charles Haberreiter
30/7	RAH HWPC	Verdi *Requiem* BBCSO Sir Malcolm Sargent
15/9	RAH HWPC*	Last Night of the Proms BBCSO Sargent
18/9	Berlin	Elgar *Gerontius* BPO Herbert Bardgett

19/9	Berlin	(repeat performance)
6/10	Gipton	Recital items A: Alan Soulsby
13/10	Wigan	Concert items
20/10	Skelmanthorpe	Concert items
25/10	Bridport	Recital A: Eric Mitchell
31/10	Bolton	*Carmen* (concert version) P.A.S. Stevens
16/11	BBC TV Bristol*	Flower Song from *Faust* (Gounod)
21/11	Plymouth	*Carmen* (concert version) William Mollineux
24/11	Tonypandy	Concert items (no details
5/12	Swindon	*Messiah* (no details)
6/12	Musselburgh	Short recital (no details)
7/12	Edinburgh	Verdi *Requiem* SNO
8/12	Glasgow	Verdi *Requiem* SNO
9/12	Manchester	*Messiah* Halle Sir John Barbirolli
19/12	Dublin	*Messiah* (no details)
22/12	Sheffield	*Messiah* (no details)
1957		
15/1	RFH	Brahms *Alto Rhapsody*; Beethoven's *Ninth*. Stanley Pope
19/1	Sheffield	Verdi *Requiem* Halle Sir John Barbirolli
31/1	RAH	Verdi *Requiem* LSO Sir Malcolm Sargent

6/2	Leningrad	Recital A: Eric Mitchell
15/2	Riga	Joint recital with Joan Hammond A: Eric Mitchell
19/2	Moscow	Recital A: Eric Mitchell
25/2	Moscow	Joint recital with Joan Hammond A: Eric Mitchell
3/3	Rawtenstall	Concert items
7/3	Carlisle	Concert items
8/3	Dumbarton	Concert items
20/3	Chatham	Concert items
25/3	Bulwell	Concert items
3/4	Leeds	Verdi *Requiem* Sir Malcolm Sargent
6/4	Wrexham	Elgar *The Music Makers* etc.
9/4	Devizes	Elgar *The Music Makers* F.V. Weaver
11/4	Petersfield	Elgar *Gerontius* Dr Sydney Watson
31/4	RAH	*Land of Hope and Glory* (RAF concert) Barbirolli
1/5	Woking	Elgar *Sea Pictures* & other items A: Eric Mitchell
8/5	Edinburgh	Opera items SNO Karl Rankl
9/5	Glasgow	(repeat of above)
11/5	Stirling	(repeat of above)
12/5	BBC London*	Three items (At Home programme) Vilem Tausky
18/5	Greenock	Opera items SNO Karl Rankl
25/5	Reading	Verdi *Requiem* Ronald Woodham

26/5	Hamilton	Concert items SNO Karl Rankl
29/5	Wigmore Hall	Five songs London Bach Group John Minchinton
2/6	Manchester	Elgar *Gerontius* Halle Sir John Barbirolli
5/6	RFH	Elgar *Gerontius* LSO Charles Groves
9/6	Dublin	Elgar *Gerontius* REO Sir John Barbirolli
14/6	Birmingham	Elgar *Sea Pictures* Sir Adrian Boult
22/6	Edinburgh	Concert items SNO Karl Rankl
6/7	Glasgow	(no details) SNO Karl Rankl (Rankl's last concert as musical director of the SNO)
29/7	Wood Green	Recital A: Eric Mitchell
4/8	Mansfield	Recital A: C.A. Taylor & Eric Mitchell
25/8	BBC London*	Three items (Grand Hotel)
8/9	Colwyn Bay	Concert items Charles Haberreiter
14/9	RAH HWPC*	Last Night of the Proms BBCSO Sargent
27/9	BBC London*	Four songs
3/10	Stroud	Concert items A: Claude Allen
9/10	Huddersfield	Concert items A: Keith Swallow
6/10	ROH	Song (ISM concert) A: Eric Mitchell
15/10	Paisley	Recital A: Eric Mitchell?

?	Addington	Recital A: Eric Mitchell?
25/10	RFH	Five items (Alamein Reunion) Band of Welsh Guards
2/11	Bulawayo	Concert items Hugh Fenn
7/11	Bulawayo	Recital A: Hugh Fenn
8/11	Salisbury	(repeat of above)
9/11	Umtali	(repeat of above)
11/11	Fort Victoria	(repeat of above)
20/11	Rome Radio*	Elgar *Gerontius* Sir John Barbirolli (First performance in Italy)
24/11	Sandbach	Concert items A: Beryl Dallen
28/11	Swansea	Concert items A: Brenda Llewellyn
6/12	Edinburgh	*Aida* (concert version) Hans Swarowsky
8/12	Carlisle	Elgar *The Music Makers* etc.
10/12	Glasgow	Concert items SNO Hans Swarowsky
12/12	RAH	Two items (Christmas concert) Ernest Read
18/12	Dublin	*Messiah* Sir John Barbirolli
22/12	Sheffield	*Messiah* Hallé Sir John Barbirolli
1958		
22/1	RAH	Verdi *Requiem* (performance abandoned)
28/1	Ayr	Concert items SNO Karl Rankl
10/2	RAH	Rubbra (new cantata - 2 performances) John Pritchard

12/2	Cheam	Concert items LSO Sir Malcolm Sargent
25/2	Manchester	Midday recital A: Eric Mitchell
26/2	Kirkaldy	Concert items SNO Hans Swarowsky
1/3	Alfreton	Recital A: Eric Mitchell
4/3	Skipton	Recital A: Eric Mitchell
8/3	Wigan	Concert items A: Eric Mitchell
9/3	New Mills	Concert items (no details)
15/3	Sheffield	Elgar *Gerontius* (no details)
28/3	Kings Lynn	Two recitals with Elsie Morison
29/3	Birkenhead	Concert items A: J. Wilfrid Clayton
6/4	Manchester	*Messiah* Halle Sir John Barbirolli
11/4	Clydebank	Concert items (Clydebank Lyric Choir)
26/4	Portsmouth	Recital with Joy Lineham
27/4	Manchester	Opera items Halle Sir John Barbirolli
28/4	Kensington	Recital with Sylvia Fisher
3/5	St Louis USA	Bach *Mass in B Minor*
9/5	Bethlehem	Bach cantatas
10/5	Bethlehem	Bach *St John Passion*
11/5	Bethlehem	Bach *Mass in B Minor*
17/5	Bethlehem	Bach *St John Passion*

18/5	Bethlehem USA	Bach *Mass in B Minor*
22/6	Australian Broadcasting Co. *	Recital (recorded for future transmission)
7/9	Melbourne	Concert for backward children
22/9	Australian Broadcasting Co.*	Interview (co-artist Jessie Matthews)
4/12	Singapore	Recital A: Noreen Stokes
13/12	Sheffield	*Messiah* Halle George Weldon
14/12	Manchester	(repeat of above)
1959		
6/1	Glasgow	Concert items SNO Karl Rankl
7/1	BBC Glasgow*	Four Scottish Songs BBC Scot Ian Whyte
7/1	Edinburgh	Concert items SNO Karl Rankl
19/1	RAH	Concert items A: Eric Mitchell
24/2	Perth	Concert items SNO Hans Swarowsky
3/3	Oldham	Concert items
7/3	Wigan	Concert items
29/3	Manchester	*Messiah* Halle Sir John Barbirolli
14/4	Bradford	Verdi *Requiem* Herbert Bardgett
15/4	Holborn	Concert items
13/5	BBC Birmingham*	Opera items
14/5	Wolverhampton	Elgar *Sea Pictures* CBSO Sir Adrian Boult

22/5	BBC Birmingham*	Elgar *Sea Pictures* CBSO Sir Adrian Boult
20/6	Edinburgh	Three items SNO Hans Swarowsky
4/7	Glasgow	(repeat of above)
18/7	Portsmouth	Recital with Joy Lineham
7/9	RAH HWPC*	Handel 'Ombra ma Fu' RPO John Hollingsworth
19/9	RAH HWPC*	Last Night of the Proms BBCSO Sargent
7/10	Northwich	Concert items A: Jenny Cadwalleder Cyril Dawes
9/10	Eastbourne	Recital with Owen Brannigan A: Eric Mitchell
14/10	Scarborough	Recital with Elsie Morison
28/10	Cheam	Concert items LSO Basil Cameron
22/11	Burnley	Concert items
2/12	Dudley	Brahms *Five Serious Songs* CBSO Meredith Davies
12/12	Tillicoultray	Concert items
17/12	Carlisle	*Carmen* (concert version) Albert Betlany
22/12	Dublin	*Messiah* Sir John Barbirolli
1960		
5/3	Bishop-wearmouth	Elgar *Gerontius*
23/3	Bolton	*Carmen* (concert version)
29/3	Brighton	Concert items

31/3	Birmingham	Verdi *Requiem* CBSO Meredith Davies
5/4	Colchester	Verdi *Requiem*
14/4	Scarborough	*Messiah*
15/4	York	*Messiah*
22/4	Larkhall	Concert items
19/5	Wigmore Hall	Recital A: Eric Mitchell
6/6	Brighton	Concert items Various brass bands A: Eric Mitchell
18/6	Edinburgh	Concert items SNO Alexander Gibson
2/7	Glasgow	Concert items SNO Gibson
8/7	Kingswinford	Recital Organist: Geoffrey Evans
10/7	Llandudno	Concert items
24/7	Worthing	Concert items
7/8	Colwyn Bay	Concert items
18/8	Herne Bay	Concert items A: Eric Mitchell
28/8	Margate	Concert items LSO Hugo Rignold
17/9	RAH HWPC*	Last Night of the Proms BBCSO Sargent
24/9	Alfreton	Recital A: Eric Mitchell
9/10	Liege, Belgium	Operatic concert
14/10	Manchester	Recital A: David Cawthra
15/10	Salford	*Aida* (concert version)
30/10	Burnley	Concert items (Police concert)

21/11	Gretna	Concert items A: James Sewell
22/11	Larkhall	Concert items
10/12	Sutton Coldfield	Recital A: Eric Mitchell
20/12	Dublin	*Messiah* John Pritchard
1961		
3/1	Edinburgh	Concert items SNO Karl Rankl
4/1	Glasgow	(repeat of above)
4/2	Batley	Concert items
15/2	Consett	Concert items
17/2	Glasgow	Songs (ICI Presentation Dinner)
29/3	Bulwell	Concert in aid of Save the Children A: Bertha Skill
1/4	Portsmouth	Concert items A: Eric Mitchell
4/4	BBC London*	Excerpt from *The Sound of Music*
8/4	Leeds	Concert items A: Ivor Newton
13/4	Blackburn	Elgar *Gerontius* Horace Tattersall

[On Monday 9 May *The Sound of Music* opened at the Palace Theatre with Constance in the role of the Mother Abbess. This virtually concluded her concert career]

24/5	Southwark Cathedral	Memorial service for Oscar Hammerstein (one item)

16/9	RAH HWPC	Last Night of the Proms BBCSO Sargent
28/9	BBC London*	Interview with Jonah Barrington 'That Reminds Me'
10/12	Woking	Concert items A: Eric Mitchell
14/12	BBC London*	Recording of 'Climb Every Mountain'
1963		
22/2	Kingston Vale	Two items Organ: Eric Mitchell
1964		
19/9	RAH HWPC	Last Night of the Proms BBCSO Sargent
[Last concert entry in Eric's ledger]		
1967		
23/9	Bulwell	Recital (last public appearance)

APPENDIX C

RECORDED MUSIC

Very few recordings of Constance's voice were ever released commercially. Those which I have been able to trace are listed below. However the British Library Sound Archive holds over thirty recordings, including performances of *Die Meistersinger* (Beecham), *Rosenkavalier* (Kleiber), *Gurreleider* (Rankl), *Peter Grimes* (Rankl), *The Beggar's Opera* (Sargent), and excerpts from *Tristan und Isolde* (Bohm) and *Messiah* (Scherchen). There are also BBC transcriptions of *Jerusalem*, the *Fantasia on British Sea Songs* and the *National Anthem*, recorded live at the last night of the 1954 Henry Wood Promenade Concerts season. For access to any of these recordings apply to The British Library, 96 Euston Road, NW1 2DB, Email: soundarchive@bl.uk

COMMERCIAL RECORDINGS:

Wagner: Love duet from *Tristan und Isolde*, Act 2 scene 2. Kirsten Flagstad, Set Svanholm, Constance Shacklock. Philharmonia Orchestra conducted by Karl Bohm. Sung in German. 78rpm. HMV DB 21112-4. Released 1950.

Handel: *Messiah*. Margaret Ritchie, Constance Shacklock, William Herbert, Richard Standon. London Symphony Orchestra conducted by Hermann Scherchen. Nixa NLP 907 - 1/3. Also Westminster WAL 308 - 3.

Gay: *The Beggar's Opera*. Elsie Morison, Monica Sinclair,

Constance Shacklock, John Cameron, Ian Wallace, Owen Brannigan, Alexander Young. Pro Arte Orchestra and Chorus conducted by Sir Malcolm Sargent. HMV CLP 1052 – 3.

The Sound of Music (excerpts). West End Cast including Shacklock. HMV mono CLP 1453, stereo CSD 1365.

Elgar, *The Dream of Gerontius*. Jon Vickers, Marian Nowakowski and Constance Shacklock. Rome Radio Orchestra and Chorus conducted by Sir John Barbirolli. Arkadia ARI 584. Issued ?1995.

Index

Alvery Lorenzo 111
Armstrong Sir Thomas 144
Arne Thomas 155
Austin Frederick 28 29 38 40

Bachauer Gina 101
Bantock Granville 33-4
Barbirolli Sir John 66 102 111 112 121 130 132
Bardgett Herbert 112
Barnes Sir Kenneth 34
Beecham Sir Thomas 55 97-8
Black Patricia 94
Blyth Alan 152
Boosey & Hawkes 41
Bowman Audrey 44
Braithwaite Lady 151-2
Braithwaite Sir Roderick 148-50
Braithwaite Warwick 150
Brannigan Owen 103
Britten Benjamin 47-8
Brook Peter 61 74-5
Burnett Muriel 44
Bush Alan 114-5
Butt Dame Clara 28

Cardus Neville 79
Coates Edith 46 55 74
Coolona Prince & Princess 48
Cooper Martin 52 104
Craxton Harold 28
Cross Joan 47

Dali Salvador 61 74-5
Dargavel Bruce 45
Davies Ryland (Rudd) 67
Doree Doris 53 54
Dowd Richard 81

Dowd Ronald 123 124
D'oyly Carte Richard 143n

Easton Neil 123
Elgar centenary 119
Evans Edgar 45 77 98 106-7
Evans Geraint 110

Ferrier Kathleen 80 108n 130
Fisher Sylvia 103 104 111 133
Flagstad Kirsten 48-51 64 143n
Fonteyn Margot 44
Franklin David 45

Gavrilkin (Russian tenor) 116
Gelhorn Peter 60 61
Glinka Michael 118
Goebbels Joseph 87
Goosens Leon 55
Greer Katharine 8
Grummer Elizabeth 96-7
Guldbaek Ruth 111

Haltrecht Montague 43-4
Hammerstein Oscar 138
Hammond Joan 8 79 112 114 115 117 118 134n
Harewood Lord 107n
Henderson Roy 21 22 24
Hislop Joseph 118
Hope-Wallace Philip 45
Hotter Hans 52 64 96
Howes Frank 60 70 83

Infantino Luigi 63
Ingleby Mona 35
Irving Ernest 38
Ivanov Yevgeni 119

Jacobs Arthur 52
Johnston James 62 100
Jones Charles 18

Karajan Herbert von 110
Kempe Rudolph 66
Kleiber Erich 8 58 102 *136* 143n 152
  telephones Constance 63-4
  conducts Wagner festival 64-5
  at ROH 65-6
  Berlin State Opera 84-9
  on Berg 104-5
  resigns Berlin post 110
  remonstrates with Legge 111
  death 110
Kleiber Ruth 68 136 *136* 152
Kovlovski Ivan 118 *134*
Kraus Otakar 127
Kubelik Rafael 109-10

Lebrecht Norman 42-3 (quoted) 109 152
Legge Walter 111 131
Lehmann Lotte 133
Leider Frida 88
Leitner Ferdinand 112 120
Lewis Bertha 23
Liddell Alvar 103
Lipatti Dinu 131-2
Litherlow Mildred 28
Llewellyn Redvers 34-5
Looser Emmy 111
Lytton Henry 23

Mackenzie Compton 113-4
Mammen Joy 122
Marchant Sir Stanley 24
Meukes Thomas 27 28
Mills Elizabeth 131
Mitchell Eric 10 53 *54* 58 62 64 89 103-4 113 114 115 121 126 127 142 143n
  helps Flagstad 50
  marriage 54-55
  in USSR 116-7
  death 141
Murphy Frank 78

Newman Ernest 45 51
Nicholas Jeremy 134n
Nilsson Birgit 111
Nillson Raymond 103 122
Notcutt Arthur 79
Nowakowski Marian 81 120

Paderewski Ignace Jan 132
Palmer Gladys 44
Partridge Miss, headmistress 18
Pears Peter 47
Phillips Linda 79
Pilarczyk Helga 127
Pinkett Eric 19
Porter Andrew 75
Potter Peter 113
Powell Mr, choirmaster 18
Powlett Sir Peveril 93

Rankl Karl 41 42 43 58 59 83 102 103 104 122
Rayment Malcolm 78 79
Redgrave Michael 133
Rodgers Richard 138 139
Rosenthal Harold 71
Rothmuller Marko *135-6*
Ross Hugh 121

Sabata Victor de 106
Sargent Sir Malcolm 82 101 102 107n 111 130 140 143n
Sargent Pamela 47-8n
Searle Humphrey 108n

Shackleton Gertrude 18
Shacklock Constance
  childhood & schooling 13-18
  musical development 18-24
  at RAM 27-32
  with CEMA 34-8
  with International Ballet 38
  joins ROH 40
  marriage *54* 55
  impressions of Rankl 59-61
  and Kleiber 66-8
  visits East Berlin 84-90
  provincial tours 90-92
  in Rhodesia 92-4
  500th ROH appearance 100
  in Buenos Aires 111-12
  at the Wexford Festival 112-4
  Russian tour 114-9
  Rome 119-20
  in USA 121
  Australian tour 122-126
  in Singapore 126
  in Liege 128 130 137
  in *Sound of Music* 139-142
  final recital 142
  joins teaching staff of RAM 144
  holiday in Soviet Union 148-52
  honours and death 154

Shacklock Frederick 13-15 18 91-2
Shacklock Hilda 10 13 14 18 19 86 91-2 147 *149*
Shacklock Rosamund 14 147 148 *149*

Shadwick Joseph 60-1
Shearer Moira 44
Sinclair Monica 113
Stephenson Dennis 103
Stevens Rise 112
Sutherland Joan 128

Taylor Charles 98
Tredaway Jean 6 7 11 12 145-6 *149 153* 154
Turner Blanche 107

Vickers Jon 98 120

Walton William 120
Weber Ludwig 87
Webster (Sir) David 47 48 49 50 53 65 94
Welitsch Ljuba 61-2
Wells H.G. 89
West Elizabeth 123
White Joan and Dennis 11
White Terry 139
Wilhelmina Queen of Netherlands 65
Williams Gwen 23
Witte Erich 127
Wood Sir Henry 32
Woofe Rousby 30-1

Young Mr, of Nottingham Co-op 21